I0412920

Alyssa Tanner

Initiation

ISBN: 9781521924440

Printed in the United States of America

First Edition

alyssa.tanner.author@gmail.com

INITIATION

An Equestrian Romance

By Alyssa Tanner

INTRODUCTION

Alyssa is back home and finds herself initiated into a lifestyle she never knew existed but one in which may be her only chance at true happiness. After years of unhappiness, a failed marriage, a number of meaningless relationships and an endless search for the fairy tale romance she so desperately desires, she comes full circle to the only place that ever felt like home. But can she bridge the gap between the love that she lost and the new one that she found?

CHAPTER 1

Alexa was standing with her back against the granite countertop, swirling a drink Mike had just handed her. Mike was busy at the island chopping vegetables for a quick stir fry. Alexa loved his attention to details and the way he took charge, making everything an experience with such flair. She swirled her drink, feeling the icy coolness of it in her hand, watching his every move.

He treated her like royalty whenever she was in town. If there was one thing she loved the most, it was his class! He knew how to treat a lady. Mike prided himself on treating her like she deserved nothing but the best. He would run her bath, filling the whirlpool tub with her favorite lavender bubbles so she could soak in peaceful bliss, making sure her glass was always full, checking on her while she soaked away the stress after long flights. He pampered her like a princess and she loved it.

He respected the high-stress, chaotic world that she worked in as a top-level marketing executive. Dating a millionaire rancher had its perks! Truth be known, after almost two years, Alexa was not only in love with the ranch and the peace it afforded her, but secretly, was in love with Mike.

"Hey Honey, what do you think about going to this new club downtown?" Mike startled her out of her daydreaming.

"Tonight?" she questioned as she stepped forward setting her glass down on the island next to his.

"Yes, tonight silly," grinning at her with the most gorgeous blue eyes that always seemed to be as playful as they were sexy.

"I thought we were staying in and having a romantic meal just the two of us?" Alexa moved closer to gently kiss his neck, reaching around his back, letting her fingers make their way from the tip of his chin, down his broad masculine chest, inching their way further with each kiss until they came to rest at the top of his well fit jeans, clearly making her intentions known.

Quickly responding to her caresses, Mike was rock hard. He leaned his head around to sensuously kiss her while playfully moving just out of reach as he tossed the skillet on to the burner. Turning up the heat he expertly tossed the ingredients in the pan like a pro.

"Nothing more I would love than to have you for dessert, right here, right now," he teased. "But there is this club downtown that I have been dying to take you to, I just wasn't sure the timing was right."

Satisfied with the progress of the meal, he switched the burner to low and engulfed her in his arms, picking her up off of her feet and setting her on the island. "I think the time is right. I think you will love it!"

Alexa and Mike had been dating for just over two years and in that time their sense and love for passion and sexual exploration had blown her mind. She had never known anyone like him before, nor ever felt the things that she did in his sensual experienced arms. And his hands, his hands could do things to her body that she never knew possible. She was blown away by the way her body reacted to his touch.

"We have been out to most of the clubs in the city. What makes this one any different?" Alexa couldn't help but pout her bottom lip in a way that she knew drove him crazy. She wanted nothing more than to skip dinner all together and go straight to dessert.

Hearing her hesitation, Mike quickly decided that maybe this wasn't the right time. Maybe he had misjudged the clues and signals that she might be open to a new adventure. But he felt deep in his heart that if she just trusted him, trusted him enough, that she would not only enjoy it, but come to love it as much as he did.

CHAPTER 2

Trying to think quickly on his feet before totally spoiling the mood, Mike grabbed for his cell phone. Scrolling through page after page he found what he was looking for and hit the forward button to send the link to Alexa's phone.

Watching Mike scroll through his phone, Alexa hopped off of the island and placed her glass under the ice dispenser preparing to fix another drink. When she was at the ranch she rarely paid her phone much attention. Being out there and away from her phone and business was all that she cared about. Being tied to her cell phone constantly was one of her biggest sources of stress. She looked over at it and let the light continue to blink. From the minute he picked her up at the airport she immediately turned the phone on silent.

"Honey, check your phone. I sent you a link I want you to see and tell me your thoughts." Mike put distance between them by crossing to the other side of the island and busied himself flipping and stirring the contents of the skillet. He wasn't ready to see the initial reaction on her face.

"Babe, what is this? What kind of club is this?" Alexa had her head down scrolling through the pages, clicking on links and just staring intently at her phone as she tried to process what she was seeing and reading. Alexa had spent her entire life travelling around the world and knew what she was seeing. Hell she had lived in Paris, been to Amsterdam and travelled all over Europe. But to imagine it here, in Denver? No way. And above all, to think of actually going to such a place, that was beyond all reasoning that her brain could process.

Yet on some deep-seated level, a strange warmth begin to pulse at the very idea. How could she possibly admit that to herself? Let alone to Mike. She was caught in her own mental tangle, grappling with desire and the fear of staring down the social norms. Never mind if her friends or business associates ever found out. This was crazy. She was crazy. Crazy for feeling so turned on by the prospect and scared out of her mind of the unknown. Real people, normal people did not do these things. Did they?

From across the island Mike was intently watching her face as her emotions were changing by the second. "Shit this was a bad idea," he chastised himself. Wishing above all else that he had never sent that link. How was he going to get out of this one gracefully? He had just ruined what he had planned as a beautiful night with the most passionate woman he had ever met.

Tripping over her own words like a high school teenager, Alexa said the first dumb thing that she could think of to overcome her shock and regain her composure. "What do they really do there?" As if she really didn't have a clue or had not read the pages, "Dammit that sounded like an idiot," she thought.

"Look, never mind. I shouldn't have suggested it. I am sorry it made you feel uncomfortable

— I never meant…" and he let his words trail off while he reached for two plates. Mike finished serving their plates and carried them into the formal dining room, leaving Alexa alone in the other room to give them both the space they needed to process this apparent faux pas.

CHAPTER 3

"What if I want to go?" Alexa threw the question out there while gently setting her wine glass on the classic antique table that dominated the spacious formal dining room. Sipping a fine slender glass of Moscato, she smiled. For all the extensive collection of expensive and vintage wines in the custom-built cellar, she always preferred a Moscato.

"What? What did you just say — Are you serious? Would you..." Mike leaned back in his chair not sure if he had heard Alexa speak those words or if his mind was just playing tricks on him.

"I don't know. I'm not sure — I mean I never thought about anything like that before — let alone actually go into a lifestyle club." Alexa stumbled for words trying to mask her growing inner excitement and outer insecurity.

"Alexa if you are not comfortable when we get there we can leave."

"Is that a promise?"

"You know it is, I would never lie to you or make you feel uncomfortable."

"It's just something I never thought of ever doing." Alexa stared down at her plate and began eating. Mike was an excellent cook and she always enjoyed whatever he dished up. Shrimp and pasta were one her favorites. She wasn't much of a vegetable eater unless she could smother them in butter or cheese, but Mike loved broccoli and cauliflower and always added them to most dishes. He was much more into healthy eating, preferring to cook at home. She was always running like an eight day clock and had a bad habit of grabbing quick convenience meals or fast-food, eating on the run. She enjoyed their meals together.

"You are always game and never back down from a challenge. That's what I have always loved so much about you," Mike said.

"What is up with this club?" Alexa questioned as she reached for her wine glass.

"I have a lot of friends Alexa that are not associated with the equestrian world. We hang out. I've been single a long time and gave up the traditional bar scene and trying to find the perfect person."

Together they both looked up and stared at each other for what seemed like a lifetime and in actuality mere minutes before Mike reached across the table to take her hands in his and squeeze them so tight Alexa felt the need surge between them.

After years of loneliness, broken marriages, endless heartache, terrible dates that felt more like train wrecks, a bond began to form between them that neither thought they would ever find in this lifetime.

Could there really be another person on this planet that truly could understand the need and want that coursed through their bodies? A need so deep that it rocked their faith… A need to feel free to express themselves in a way that Alexa had never known or been free to express, let alone feel or share with anyone.

CHAPTER 4

As Alexa jumped in the shower her mind was racing. One minute she was overcome with the wildly crazy idea of actually getting to explore her own sexuality with a man she dearly loved, and the next, she was near panic with the fear of the unknown.

"What if I panic? What if I hate it?" Her pulse raced as her mind played a thousand what ifs. "What if I lose him forever?" And that fear gripped her deep in her chest threatening to choke off the very life that she had only hours ago dreamed for.

After two years of trying so hard to keep her heart in check and remain level-headed about their relationship, she knew that tonight could very well turn into a complete disaster. They weren't two teenagers; they were in the prime of their lives. Both with well-established careers and they each craved their freedom as much as the other. Where most couples couldn't handle long-distance relationships, it had worked perfectly for them. They missed each other dearly while apart and made up for it whenever they could.

The weekends that they spent together were whirlwinds of fun, uninhibited, raw, passionate, sex that knew no bounds. They could spend hours in bed cuddling and snuggling, recuperating from the last marathon session, only to wake up and be just as aroused. It might only take a whisper or the low touch of his hand to have her craving him all over again.

Alexa had had her share of great lovers in the past but none had ever been able to make her entire body convulse uncontrollably with just his hands. Their bodies seemed made for each other. Her pleasure always came first to Mike. Not until she was nearly spent and thought that she couldn't possibly orgasm again would he finally take her over the edge. The soft whispers in her ears encouraging her every move, the feeling of his powerful muscular body engulfing her from behind, pushed her higher and higher as she rode each wave of orgasm that rippled throughout her body.

When she could barely breathe, let alone speak would he finally speed up the pace, thrusting so deep inside of her that she could feel his need for release. They would both come together in what seemed like a fierce and powerful explosion off the top of a mountain. Then came the free-falling; the sheer weightless bliss that overtook them as they collapsed into each other's arms amidst gentle murmurs as they slept, was a feeling like no other.

Alexa snapped out of it as she heard Mike calling her from the bedroom. "Are you ok in there?"

She had no idea how long she had been standing beneath the steaming water, letting it wash over her, trying to clear her mind. She hadn't even touched the shampoo yet.

"Just a few more minutes," she quickly answered him as she frantically grabbed the shampoo. "Damn, now I am going to be late and he is going to think I am stalling." Which maybe in a way she was, stalling the inevitable, subconsciously buying her some time.

CHAPTER 5

Outside Mike already had the truck running and was putting a zippered leather bag behind the driver's seat. Alexa was glad that they were taking the truck instead of the car. On a hot summer day she loved riding with the top down feeling the wind and sun on her face. But tonight she was thankful that he had decided to take the truck instead. More room, more space. Space she desperately needed at the moment in order to regain control of her emotions.

She still didn't know exactly how she felt about this strange unexpected twist of events. Would she blow it?

Ever the gentleman, Mike quickly came around to the passenger side and opened her door. He gave her the sexiest grin as she gracefully stepped up onto the slender running board, which always proved a tricky feat when she was dressed up and wearing 3 inch heels. She tossed her purse on the floor board and set her travel mug into the console.

Still holding the door open, Mike let her get situated before he lightly placed his hand on her bare thigh, letting it drift across her skin, gently squeezing the sensitive spot just above her knee.

"It is going to be fine. You are fine and that is all that matters."

Alexa settled deeper into the seat feeling the cool leather against her nearly bare bottom. Her legs trembled slightly and a shiver ran up her spine. The short black leather skirt she was wearing had been an impulse-buy on one of their previous trips. She had spotted it amongst tons of racks and knew she had to have it. She loved the feeling of the leather against her skin.

Alexa wasn't one to dress sexy or provocative, much preferring her jeans, t-shirts and sandals.

She lived her life in power suits at work and enjoyed stripping them off as soon as she hit the front door, swapping them for comfortable bum around attire that consisted of jeans or yoga pants with a baggy t-shirt.

Elegant ball gowns were the exception and she had a closet full. When the occasion called for it, she loved dressing up to the hilt. She would spend hours getting ready. Her shoulder length wavy reddish brown hair, compliments of her Irish ancestors, took the majority of time to style with perfection. A stray curl here or there could cause her fits. Eventually she would give in and let it fall where it did.

Sitting in her robe at her dressing table she enjoyed the art of putting on her make-up, paying attention to each detail. She had never liked the painted on look and always opted for a fresh, barely there look, which could be harder to achieve then it sounded.

To Alexa it was like playing dress-up as a kid. A fairytale make believe fantasy come true. Yes, she secretly enjoyed the ritual and thrill of extravagant parties and the many balls that were part of her social life back home.

But the uber short leather mini skirt and tight fitting tank top was foreign to her. The feeling of the cool leather on her bare skin sent a chill up her spine. She had never felt comfortable going out in the cute, sexy outfits that her girlfriends loved to wear. It just wasn't her.

"Are you sure you are ok?" She heard Mike say, yanking her out of her mental safe place.

"Yes, really. I'm fine."

"That doesn't sound like a very confident answer."

"Seriously, I'm good." Alexa reached over to the console for her tumbler that she had personally spiked before leaving the house. She needed the liquid courage.

"Alexa there is no pressure. Honestly. It is a very upscale club. The main floor has a huge dance floor and a DJ. We can just hang out like any other club if you don't feel comfortable."

She swirled the ice cold tumbler in her right hand, staring out of the windshield at the beautiful night sky with the city lights far off in the distance.

She could feel Mike take her left hand in his and gently press it to his lips.

"Dammit," she thought. She loved him more than she would even dare to admit, even to herself. But at this moment she felt like a first date with a stranger. She didn't want to lose him, not after the last two years. He had become her world. Her knight in shining armor and she had started to believe that maybe fairytales did come true.

Mike tapped a button on the steering wheel filling the truck with one of their favorite romantic playlists and she eased back in her seat as he sped up the ramp onto the interstate.

CHAPTER 6

As Mike eased the truck into the parking lot, Alexa couldn't help but stare at the line of Limos stretched out front.

"You are parked in the VIP section."

"Yes."

"You have a membership?"

"Take off your panties." Mike said as he backed into a VIP slot.

"You are kidding right?" Alexa said in a voice that sounded closer to cry for help instead of a question.

"Slip them off and leave them in the truck," Mike answered as he reached in the backseat for the leather bag. "Just trust me. Please, just this once."

"Trust you? Mike I have trusted you my whole life. But this? This is on an entirely new level."

Mike had been her trainer, her coach and her friend. Mike had introduced her to the equestrian sport of dressage and she had immediately fallen in love with the sport spending countless hours practicing and perfecting the intricate patterns and movements that defined each level.

Alexa had grown up in the world of dressage and still loved it. She hadn't ridden in years but being back at the ranch surrounded by the horses and riders was comforting.

Dressage at its very core was a partnership between horse and rider. To become an elite competitor required a rider to have and maintain complete control at all times, but it also required absolute trust between the two. It was a beautiful dance of lead and follow with the strength and power of the animal harnessed and shown in all of its graceful glory.

At 6ft, 4 inches, Mike made an impressive sight dressed in the skin-tight breeches and tailored waistcoat that were traditional of the sport. When he removed his top hat and waved to the crowd it was hard for every female watching not to wish those deep blue eyes were trained on her.

Mike had built an empire raising and training high dollar equestrian mounts and he was one of the most respected and sought after trainers and rider in the business. She had always trusted his guidance and he had never steered her wrong. She had him to thank for the years that she spent in a sport she dearly loved and enjoyed.

"But this? What the hell was this? Who was this person sitting next to her?" Alexa's thoughts were all over the place. "And what in the hell was she doing here?" When he first brought it up at dinner she had thought it might be fun and exciting, now she was thinking that this was a really bad idea.

Alexa was still clutching her drink with both hands when Mike opened her door.

Mike gently slid her drink from her hands and reached in to unbuckle her seatbelt. Setting the tumbler back into the console, he took her hand and helped her out of her seat.

As she stood up out of the vehicle, Mike spoke quietly in her ear, "Turn around Honey," and she felt the warmth of his hands reach up under her skirt and slowly slip her black lace tangas down her bare legs, careful not to catch the lace on her heels, tucking them into the side pocket on the door.

Mike gave her his most sexy smile that he knew had always made her heart melt as he closed the door and hit the remote locking the vehicle for the night. "Ready?"

Mike slid his arm around her waist as he escorted her up the slight incline toward the entrance. Alexa spotted the red carpet and the elegantly dressed doormen that looked like they had just stepped off the cover of a GQ magazine.

As they reached the entrance the two doormen expertly greeted them like they were walking into the classiest five-star hotel. Mike placed his hand on her lower back and guided her through the beautifully ornate doors, and into a world that she knew nothing about.

At the front desk, Alexa could hear the music playing and see people sitting at tables mingling.

She could see the reflections of the colored strobe lights in the full length mirrors along the wall

Over her left shoulder she could see Mike signing them in and couldn't help but notice the tall, slender gorgeous hostess who had skin the color of caramel. Her long brown hair was perfectly straightened and she had the most gracious, pleasant smile as she nodded to Alexa, motioning for her to step up to the counter.

"Welcome to the club," she said to Alexa. "I just need you to sign right here and you are all set. Tonight is 'No Panty Friday' and all bare-bottom ladies get in free." Her voice was as smooth as silk and had an inviting, calming tone that made her very good at her job. It took the edge off of Alexa's frigid flight and fear mode.

She smiled at Alexa as she spoke. "Shall we begin the tour?"

It was obvious that she had been well trained on the nuances of making first time patrons feel at home. She gracefully stepped from behind the counter and led them out into the main dance floor area, pointing out the location of the bar, dance floor, and restrooms while casually interjecting the rules and guidelines of the club.

Mike held Alexa's hand as he trailed a step behind her allowing her to follow the hostess toward the VIP areas.

"On our left we have the VIP room that can be reserved for private parties," she continued like a top-notch real-estate salesperson.

Alexa continued to follow her as she led them to the ornate winding staircase that led to the second floor. Mike was right behind her and he playfully ran his hand up under her skirt. She could feel the warmth of his hand on her bare bottom and despite all of her reserves; her body instinctively reacted to his touch.

She could feel the warm, aching sensation that just begged for the feeling of his fingers deep inside of her. Her body betrayed her mind as she could feel the liquid heat starting to flow.

"And down this hall we have the semi-private rooms," the hostess said as she held back one of the sheer curtains, snapping Alexa's mind back into focus.

The hostess continued escorting them through the various areas, explaining the etiquette, rules, and guidelines as they moved from one area to the next.

Finding themselves back where they began, Alexa listened as the hostess wrapped up the tour.

"If you have any questions or need any-thing, please feel free to ask any one of our staff members and they will gladly assist you. We want you to have a pleasant and enjoyable experience here with us tonight."

As the hostess stepped around them, she lightly rubbed Alexa's shoulder. "Relax and enjoy. It is all about being free to be yourself. Again, wel-come to the club."

CHAPTER 7

F inally free to explore the club on their own they made their way down the spiral staircase to the Main floor. Alexa wanted a drink so they headed for the bar. The club was BYOB and Mike had given the bartender the two bottles of Moscato to put on ice before they started the tour.

As Mike poured them each a glass, Alexa was studying the dance floor area. There were raised platforms of different heights along one side of the dance floor. The wall behind the dance floor was a solid mirror. In the opposite corner was an elevated stage area complete with a silver stripper pole that reflected the colors of the spinning strobe lights and mirror ball.

"Here you go Honey," Mike said, handing her the slender wine glass. "What do you think?"

"Unbelievable," she answered him, taking a slow sip, letting the cool sweet wine wet her lips.

"The club, or the fact that you are here?"

"Both."

"Why don't we find a table and watch the action for a little while." Mike picked up his glass and slid his arm around Alexa's waist hugging her to his chest.

"Sounds like a plan..." Alexa let him lead their way to the nearest table.

As they settled into the overstuffed round back armchairs Alexa studied the room. It was large and spacious with tables and chairs surrounding the dance floor. On the back wall near the DJ booth there were tall round tables designed to stand around. There were several near the bar area as well.

The club was packed and she couldn't help but notice the single guys that were interspersed here and there, mostly standing around the tall tables, some leaning on the bar watching the action.

Single men were only allowed in the club on certain nights and they could only enter the VIP areas if invited by a member to join them. The club was specifically designed for couples as a safe and fun place to entertain their own sexuality with other like-minded couples.

Alexa noticed as a tall blonde stood up from the table where she had been sitting with her partner, kissing him as she bent over to pick-up her glass from the table. Dressed in a gorgeous slinky, emerald green short dress that scooped down in the front showing off enough cleavage to definitely get attention, but stopping short of exposing her nipples.

The slender blonde glided across the floor like a runway model as she headed for one of the tall tables. Alexa watched as the blonde approached a tall black haired guy that had been intently watching her from across the room. The blonde sexily slowed her pace as she neared the table. Setting her glass down on the table, she ran her hand up the back of his neck letting her fingers comb through his dark hair. They spoke for a few minutes before grabbing their glasses and heading towards the staircase.

Alexa's mouth dropped open and she was glad that she had not just taken a sip at that moment. She looked over at Mike in astonishment, only to see him grinning like a Cheshire cat.

"She just made his night, or will as soon as they get upstairs."

"Mike this is nuts! She just left her partner sitting at a table and picked-up a single guy right in front of him."

"Relax Honey, just watch..." Mike squeezed her hand and reached for his glass with the other.

Alexa trained her eyes on the man that had obviously just been dumped in front of everyone expecting to see him jump out of his chair in a fit. Instead of storming out of the club, the man slowly rose from his chair, reached for his drink and headed towards the stairs.

"Oh this isn't going to be good," she blurted out.

Mike just grinned.

"Relax, that is their thing. There isn't going to be trouble. This isn't your typical nightclub."

"Their thing?" Alexa almost choked.

"Yes. Some men find it a huge turn-on to watch their partner seduce a stranger. It is part of the acting out of their fantasies. That is what the lifestyle is all about. She isn't cheating behind his back. He will give them some time to bond and heat up the action, and then he will either join them or be content to just watch."

"Are you nuts?"

"Honey, if you did something like that for me I would lose my mind with excitement."

"Oh this is absolutely crazy! I need another drink or two or three."

"Let's go walk and we can stop at the bar to refill our drinks before heading upstairs." Easing out of his chair, Mike slid Alexa's chair back and reached out for her hand

The theatre room was softly lit with long white leather couches arranged around the room to allow couples to mingle or settle in and enjoy some personal time. The huge wall to wall television screen at the far end was playing various adult movies to set the mood.

When they entered the room Alexa had a strange sense of excitement and peace that she couldn't describe. There were couples settled in different areas, some visiting and talking, others enjoying their partners either cuddling or watching the movie or actively engaging in their own pleasure.

To say that Alexa was extremely turned on by the atmosphere would be a huge understatement. It was nothing like she had imagined. A strange mental shift began happening in her brain as she took in the sights and sounds around her. It was like the slow crumbling of an ingrained taboo that had imprisoned her entire adult life.

The couples were well dressed and well mannered. This was nothing like she had imagined, or feared. These couples were relaxing, sipping wine from slender fluted glasses while they expressed their most intimate loving selves in such an open way that it calmed her nervous anxiety in a way that she had not expected at all

Mike held her hand and kissed her softly on her cheek, allowing her to just process her own mental thoughts. She leaned her back into his chest, letting him embrace her as a familiar warmth began spreading through her body. She had never imagined being so turned on in this way.

As she relaxed in his arms she heard him ask, "Everything ok Honey?"

"Yes, it is beautiful — excitingly beautiful — I mean exciting in a beautiful way," she stammered trying to find the right words while keeping her intimate thoughts in check. How could she admit just how turned on she really was? What would Mike think of her? Was this some sort of weird crazy test of her loyalty?

Sure she had watched adult movies together with other guys she dated, but porn wasn't her thing. Oh it excited her and got the job done but there was always this twisted, guilty, ugly feeling afterward. She wasn't like those women and it left her feeling like her partner wasn't making love to her but to some fantasy porn star in the movie. She just didn't like that feeling.

But the couples in the room were very, very different — they were real. Real couples, who were interacting with and enjoying their partners in such an intimate and open manner that it seemed natural, actually the seats near the screen were mostly empty. Instead, most of the couples were on the other side of the room in a more intimate setting, gathering and talking with other couples. Some of the couples were alone enjoying their own intimate pleasures, while others were just leisurely watching the action. The atmosphere in the room was intoxicating and Alexa was beginning to feel the effects that it sparked inside of her.

Alexa tuned around in Mike's embrace to face him and reached up to kiss him. "Can we sit down?"

"That's my girl!" Mike answered her as he let her lead the way to a spot in the corner where there was room to get comfortable.

Alexa found herself getting hotter and hotter by the minute as she watched the other couples passionately kissing and caressing one another.

Alexa cuddled up into Mike's arms and started massaging his shoulders and working her way across his chest. She nibbled playfully at his ears and kissed his neck, getting bolder and bolder as the sounds of the other couples started to feed her mind with wild thoughts. She could feel Mike's hand slide between her thighs gently stroking her skin as he inched closer and closer to the center of her aching desire.

With every movement of his hand she let her thighs part wider until the constraints of the tight leather skirt reached its limit. Mike could always drive her completely crazy this way and he knew it. The aching need and desire to have his hands work their magic was almost more than she could stand and the sounds and sights fell out of her consciousness as she closed her eyes, enjoying every touch.

On the verge of losing control and succumbing to his sensuous touches, she suddenly felt Mike withdraw his hand and straighten her skirt.

"Not yet Honey."

Alexa groaned as she tried to catch her breath, suddenly becoming aware of the other couples in the room that had been watching them play.

With her still straddling his hips, Mike stood up and let her slide down his body setting her on her feet.

CHAPTER 8

Together they walked back down the hallway leading to the private room area. On one side of the hall were the doors to the private rooms. People were mingling in the hallway and the excitement seemed to be coming from further down and across the hall.

Mike took the lead this time and holding her hand they weaved their way through the crowd towards the direction of the noise emanating from the group playroom. The door to the room was open but it wouldn't have mattered because there was a large window cutout in the wall, wide enough that six or seven people could stand shoulder to shoulder to watch.

This was definitely the center of attention! There were people mingling and talking in the hall, while others took turns at the window, resting their elbows on the ledge or hugging each other while they watched.

Several people smiled at Alexa as she followed Mike through the group. Alexa became very aware that these people were genuinely, and openly welcoming. So much unlike the snobbish cliques that dominated the social gatherings she was used of attending. No fake smiles or fake laughs. Absent was the condescending pecking order and clannish attitude.

As Mike finally made his way to the viewing area, one couple turned sideways creating a space for them to stand at the window.

"Here Honey, you can stand next to us. They are playing hot tonight. You don't want to miss this action," a woman in a gorgeous deep purple dress said, as she moved aside and encouraged Alexa to step into the space she had created. Her husband reached around Alexa's back to shake hands with Mike and introduce himself.

In the center of the room was a large round, white padded leather platform big enough for at least six to eight people. The walls surrounding it were lined with white leather sofas with plush throw pillows, obviously meant for comfort as well as support. The room was dimly lit from above by a large chandelier and table lamps lit the corners that separated the sectional sofas. Stacks of white plush towels were placed on the tables in the corners that held the lamps.

There were people arranged on the long sofas in all sorts of arrangements from couples to threesomes all excitedly engaging in some form of sexual activity or another. People were taking turns going in and out of the room to give others that wished a chance to get in on the action. But the main attraction was the round platform bed in the center of the room.

Alexa remembered the words the hostess had said, "If you are on the platform, consider yourself tapped-in and fair game to play." She apparently wasn't joking because from what Alexa could see it was a tangle of arms, legs and various body parts in every direction. It was hard to keep up with who was where or doing what. But from the sounds coming from the room it was obvious they were having a ball. As soon as one person would get off the bed, another would dive in and take their place.

The girl standing next to her introduced herself, "Hi I'm Leza," she said, tenderly squeezing Alexa's arm as she spoke. "I told you girl. They are on fire tonight and in rare form. It was dead in here an hour ago but things have sure heated up quick."

"Do you guys come here often?" Alexa asked.

"We love it here." Leza replied.

"Is it always like this?"

"Let me guess, this is your first time right?"

Alexa just nodded her head.

"So, what do you think?" Leza asked, giving Alexa an honest look that showed that she really cared what Alexa was thinking.

"I am honestly not sure."

"So you are new to the lifestyle as well as the club?"

"I never even imagined this in my wildest dreams. Not for real, with real people. I guess I thought it just existed in adult movies or maybe college frat houses," Alexa had to laugh at that thought.

"Well I am proud of you for being brave enough to face the unknown and come here tonight with an open mind. And if anyone hasn't yet, then let me be the first to welcome you into a lifestyle where you are free to be yourself and explore your own sexuality and fantasies without fear of judgment or condemnation."

"Is it that obvious? Do I have newbie written all over my forehead?" Alexa joked.

"Only in invisible ink. We have all been right where you are right now. We know and understand what it is like to face your fears the first time. And if you weren't half interested or the least bit aroused, you would have grabbed your man and bolted for the door by now," Leza said with a huge smile on her face.

"You are right, I am and that's the problem," Alexa whispered, trying to keep Mike from overhearing her.

"Problem? My friend you need to let it go. All that BS they have been feeding us for years about nice girls don't do such things, is just plain bullshit."

Mike had been standing behind Alexa the whole time, his arms wrapped around her waist as he watched the action in the room. As he held her tighter she could feel his arousal pressing against her back. He had not once interrupted her and Leza's conversation and even now was just holding her without saying a word.

Leza leaned in closer and whispered in her ear, "Girl we are about to fix your problem so that you can relax and enjoy yourself."

Addressing the guys this time, Leza said, "Why don't we find a seat and get comfortable?"

Mike was the first one to turn to Leza with a huge smile on his face that had Thank-you written all over it as he hugged Alexa so tight he could hear her catch her breathe.

With Leza taking the lead, the four of them wove their way into the room and found a spot along one of the sofas closer to the action on the platform. The guys were intently watching the writhing tangle of hot, sexy action taking place while Leza leaned over to Alexa to whisper, "What do you think of the view from this angle?"

"I think I like it," Alexa said, giving Leza a wicked grin.

"Told you. It doesn't get any better than this…unless you jump in."

"That, I don't think I am quite ready for…yet."

"Oh you will be, trust me." Leza softly brushed her hand along Alexa's thigh before turning to her husband.

Alexa was stunned for a moment, not sure what to think when her body reacted to Leza's touch. When she turned to Mike he was watching her with a devilishly sexy grin. Putting his arm around her waist he leaned her into his shoulder until she was almost lying across his lap while he brought his lips down to hers. Alexa was lost in his deep passionate kisses that crushed her lips with the intensity and she couldn't get enough of it. She was so turned on by the sounds of the other couples that she became engrossed in her own arousal letting her inhibitions melt away.

She could feel Mike getting rock hard beneath her shoulder and she wanted so bad to relieve that pressure. She slowly let her hands caress his chest as he ran his fingers through her long hair.

"Not yet Baby Girl, not yet," Mike said as he gently rolled her over so that she was lying on her back across his lap as he began rubbing her shoulders, playing with her hair and gently stroking her face.

Turning away from her husband, Leza grinned over at Mike and he nodded his head and returned the grin.

Mike ran his hand under Alexa's shirt caressing her bare skin, working his way up to cup her bare breast in his palm as Leza began first at her ankles and worked her way up Alexa's thighs.

Alexa began to softly moan and arched her back yielding to her bodies desire to be closer and closer to the hands that were beginning to drive her wild. She had already been so turned on by Mike's action in the theatre that her body was now aching and throbbing with a need to release all of the built up tension coiled deep inside.

She didn't care if a hundred people were watching at that moment. She needed Mike to take her over the edge until she released all of her desire and passion with each rippling climax.

But it was Leza's hands that were working the magic as Mike raised her shirt to massage her breast, firmly gripping and teasing first one nipple, then the other. Easing his hands down along her stomach, Mike eased her skirt up around her waist freeing Alexa's thighs while giving Leza more access to maneuver into position.

As Alexa felt Leza's warm lips touch her most intimate places Alexa began to come undone and could no longer hold back the pulsating spasms that overtook her. Mike cradled her in his arms as each orgasm rippled through her body, running his fingers through her long hair, he whispered words of encouragement as he held her until he felt her body go limp with sheer pleasure; letting go of all her inhibitions and yielding to Leza's passionate and tender motions.

Alexa'a body continued to tremble with each aftershock that coursed through her and she curled up into Mike's arms savoring each and every electrifying impulse.

CHAPTER 9

Alexa's head was still spinning with the after effects when Mike covered her lips with his, spreading them apart and using his tongue to reach the deepest parts, breathing life back into her as she regained her awareness of the other couples and sounds in the room. Her legs still felt like jelly as she pulled herself up into his arms straddling his lap. Holding onto the back of his head she returned each and every swirl of his tongue, pulling him closer and harder with each passionate kiss.

Alexa's body was on fire and beneath her Mike was so hard so could feel him throbbing against his jeans. She wanted Mike and she wanted him now. She needed him! She wanted him to thrust his hand deep inside of her and make her explode before taking her from behind. She craved the way that he made love to her and she needed to feel him inside of her, now!

Alexa reached between her legs to undo the button of his jeans but Mike had already anticipated her move and stood up with her in his arms before she could release the object of her desire.

Setting her on her feet, Mike whispered, "Not yet Honey, not yet. We are going to make this last until you can't resist it anymore."

Groaning deep in her throat Alexa was still on fire. Glancing down at the couples piled on the platform only ignited the flames inside of her even more.

Straightening her skirt and brushing back her hair with his fingers Mike steadied her on her feet before leading them back out into the hallway.

She saw Mike glance up and down the hallway at the private rooms but all of the doors were closed indicating that they were currently being used by other couples seeking a private space to play.

"This is going to have to do Honey," Mike said as he backed her up to one of the walls in a space between two doors of the private rooms. "Turn around Honey."

At that precise moment Alexa could have cared less if the entire world was watching. She needed Mike and she needed him now. Turning around in his arms so that he stood directly behind her, Alexa spread her feet apart balancing on the slender three-inch spiked heels and moaned as she felt his hand reach around her and slip beneath her skirt.

What Mike could do to her body with just his hands was unlike anything she had ever experienced before.

To someone who had never felt that kind of orgasmic release in their lives they may have been stunned, shocked or even shamed into embarrassment, but Alexa knew well the intense, incredible release that would have her body convulsing in wave after wave of rhythmic pulses that involuntarily took over, leaving her reeling with the most powerful, blissful feeling in the world.

As she firmly planted both of her trembling hands flat against the wall, trying to keep her balance, she could feel the rush of her orgasm running down her legs, soaking her sandals and leaving her standing in a puddle only seconds before the next wave coursed through her body and her trembling legs went limp.

The utter sensation of free falling into a weightless spiral was like no other and she let herself slip into Mike's powerful arms as he caught her around her waist and held her in his arms, her head falling onto his shoulder as the endorphins flooded through her body.

Mike held Alexa in his arms gently cradling her against his shoulder, kissing the top of her head softly, not wanting to rouse her from her bliss until she had fully recovered.

Lost in her own spinning world of sheer pleasure Alexa barely heard someone say, "Damn, now that is hot!"

Mike was still holding her steady as the trembling in her legs began to subside and she could finally feel her feet again.

"That was impressive," Alexa heard someone else say as they patted Mike on the back.

Alexa turned around to see Mike looking down at her with a sexy, wicked grin.

"That's my girl," Mike whispered as he gathered her into his arms.

CHAPTER 10

"Thirsty?" Mike grinned as he ushered Alexa back down the long hallway towards the stairs.

Alexa wasn't sure she could navigate the winding staircase on her wobbly legs that still felt like jelly but she was dying of thirst. Mike knew what he did to her and just how fast she dehydrated during their endless love making sessions.

At the bar, Mike refilled their glasses and ordered a large glass of ice water for Alexa.

Alexa quickly took the glass of water that Mike held out for her as he carried their wine glasses and headed towards one of the tall tables.

Alexa took a huge gulp of water and let the crushed ice melt on her tongue cooling and quenching her thirst. The wine was way too sweet just yet and she continued to indulge herself in the ice cold water to cool down.

The dance floor had heated up and there were several couples dancing together and even a slender brunette up on the platform with the pole. Across the room Alexa spotted Leza and Ricardo talking to another couple. As soon as Leza spotted Mike and Alexa, she and Ricardo along with the other couple began making their way across the room to join them.

Ricardo shook Mike's hand and introduced him to the other couple.

"Girl, for a newbie that was some pretty hot stuff up there," Leza whispered to Alexa.

Remembering how it started Alexa blushed a bright red color and could feel the heat on her face.

"Let's take a walk and I will show you where the restrooms are so you can freshen up," Leza turned to the group and said, "We will be right back, just going to the lady's room."

As they walked away from the table Alexa grabbed Leza's forearm and stammered for words. "Leza I have never done anything like that before…"

"Never even thought about it?"

"Well yeah, sort of but not really. I am mean — not really actually doing it." Alexa blushed even more.

"It is called bicurious and there is absolutely nothing in the world wrong about that. You need to let go of all the mental inhibitions holding you back from experiencing whatever you wish to experience. That is why we come here, to be around and socialize with other couples who share the same views."

"But how do you deal with not feeling guilty or jealous?"

"Guilty of what? You come here as a couple and mutually consent to explore your own sexuality. All of us set our own personal boundaries both individually and as a couple and we talk about it. You aren't doing anything behind each other's back. There is nothing to be guilty of."

"And you don't get jealous?"

"Oh jealousy is a part of being human and of course it creeps up on you from time to time, but you learn to handle it and deal with it and that is what makes the bond between you and your partner even stronger. Some of the couples here tonight are not just threesomes for the night."

"What?" Alexa almost dropped her glass.

"They are threesomes by choice and live and love together on a permanent basis. Not always in the same house but some do. It is called consensual non-monogamy, or as they call it in the lifestyle, polyamorous."

"You are flipping kidding me, right?"

"Not at all."

"What?"

"The three partners often have very different personalities, styles, tastes, you name it, but together it works for them. They very often love each other in very different ways. It isn't a competition. It is more of a symbiotic relationship between three consenting adults."

"That is crazy!"

"Really? How so? How many cheating couples have you known in your lifetime that have a wife at home and a mistress across town? Or vice versa?"

"But…"

"But nothing. These couples aren't cheating behind each other's back or trying to tear apart another's relationship. They love each other equally, openly, and honestly. It may not be for everybody but that is what this lifestyle is about. People can be free to be who they are and love how they wish without shame or condemnation."

"I don't know. I don't know if I could handle it — I mean once was an awesome experience but…"

"But nothing, if he wants to cheat on you he will do that anyhow so why be at home alone driving yourself crazy thinking about it. You know who you came here with and you know who you are going home with at the end of the night."

"True, but this whole thing is a lot to process…"

"Alexa you were hot as hell up there tonight and had everyone's attention. If Mike is crazy enough to mess up and lose you then he is an idiot!"

CHAPTER 11

"Honey that was the most incredible night of my life watching you enjoy yourself to the absolute fullest. I have brought other dates to the club before, but never and I mean never have I been so turned on as I was tonight being there with you. You are incredible."

"It was an incredible night."

"I'll say. You looked like you were really enjoying yourself."

"I did. I have never experienced anything like that before."

"So how did you like Leza?" Mike questioned with a grin on his face.

Alexa immediately felt her face go flush and she fumbled in the console for an earring she had dropped.

"Alexa, look at me Honey. There is nothing wrong with anything that happened tonight. You were beautiful and brave and let yourself enjoy every minute of the experience. There is no faking that level of passion and expression. It was beautiful just watching you let yourself go."

"Are you being honest?"

"Damn straight I am being honest. I feel like the luckiest man on the planet. Every man in that place had his eyes on you."

"And that doesn't bother you?"

"Bother me? Are you kidding? I loved every minute of it. It makes me hard as a rock just thinking about it."

"I feel bad because I left you hanging. I wanted us to enjoy it together."

"As soon as we get home Honey, I'll have my turn, trust me. Tonight was all about you and giving you a chance to really let go of all of your inhibitions and being free to explore and enjoy your own passion and sexuality."

Alexa loved the feel and taste of taking Mike in her mouth, the sensation of his velvety skin contrasting with the rock hard stiffness that yielded to her every stroke. She loved feeling the veins rubbing against her tongue as she slowly slid her lips down his entire length, taking him all in and swirling her tongue around as she gently pulled back driving him crazy.

She loved the way Mike held her hair back so that he could watch her. To Alexa it showed respect and encouraged her to keep going, increasing her speed at times and then slowing it down to prolong his enjoyment. She would ever so gently slide him slowly out until she was only kissing and swirling the very tip. She loved it. She loved knowing he was so turned on by hearing the soft moans coming from deep in his throat as she teased the most sensitive part of his erection. Tasting that first drop of excitement turned her on to no end and she would quickly open her moth wide to allow him to thrust his full length into her before wrapping her lips fully around him.

She could drive him to madness by prolonging his pleasure. Paying attention to every move and sound he made. If there is one thing Mike could be sure of, it was that she never started something she didn't intend to finish until the end. Giving him pleasure was a joy in itself and feeling him release everything he had into her was the ultimate reward.

Their bodies seemed to be made for each other. Her pleasure always came first to Mike. Not until she was nearly spent and thought that she couldn't possibly orgasm again would he finally take her over the edge.

The soft whispers in her ear encouraging her every move, the feeling of his powerful, muscular body engulfing her from behind, pushed her higher and higher as she rode each wave of orgasm that rippled throughout her body.

When she could barely breathe, let alone speak he would speed up the pace, thrusting so deep inside of her that she could feel his need for release. They would both come together in what seemed like a fierce and powerful explosion off the top of a mountain.

Then came the free-falling, the sheer weightless bliss that overtook them as they collapsed into each other's arms amidst the gentle murmurs as they drifted off to sleep.

CHAPTER 12

A lexa was out on the terrace over-
looking the stables and rolling hills
that stretched out as far as she could
see. Still in her robe, she was sipping her first cup
of coffee and enjoying the early morning breeze.
This was her favorite time of the day. Watching the
sun rise over the hills, the early morning dew creating a misty haze that seemed to her like a fantasy
world of dreams, always made her feel at peace.
She loved it here and had missed it more than she
dared admit.

"You are so flipping beautiful Alexa. I never get tired of watching you," Mike softly answered.
"You have no idea what you do to me."

"Good Morning, Honey. What are you do-
ing up so early?" Alexa tilted her head back to kiss
him as he leaned over her, rubbing her shoulders.

"Enjoying the view."

"The view…"

"Ever since you were a kid I loved watching you ride. Your grace, your style, and the way
you just seemed to glide even through the most dif-
ficult moves."

Alexa gave him a sideways glance that was
more of an unspoken question.

"No, not like that at all. I mean back then I
just knew that there was something so special about
you. The way that you carried yourself, your confidence and determination was fascinating. I never
once in my wildest dreams thought that one day we
would be together. Seeing you sitting out here,
looking so relaxed and peaceful reminds me of just
how lucky I am."

As her dressage coach and trainer, she had
looked up to Mike and admired him ever since she
could remember.

Her aspirations and dreams of competing at
the Olympic level had been cut short when she had

lost her beloved gray Andalusian mare Gabri to a freak accident. It was also the same summer she had lost her virginity and her heart to her first love. By the end of that summer Alexa had decided to walk away from the sport forever and never rode again.

She swore to herself that no one and nothing would ever get that close to her heart again. The devastating heartbreak of losing both the loves of her life was too much. All that she had ever dreamed of had been ripped away from her in one tragic night. With her no longer competing or riding, her and Mike had just drifted out of each other's lives.

Mike had taught her to ride and introduced her to the world of dressage and she had fallen in love with the sport immediately. Watching him ride in competition just left her in awe. She wanted to be that good. To compete and win at that level was a dream.

She loved seeing him in his riding breeches, immaculate white shirt, coat and tails, and the gorgeous top hat he wore made an unmistakable impression on her.

Alexa grew up on fairytales of knights on white horses riding off to battle, returning home to rescue the love of their lives and live happily ever after. As a kid she had believed those fairy tales could come true. She was always an avid reader and as a teenager she had engrossed herself in countless romance novels to escape her own reality. Lost in another world, she could escape into a fantasy world far different than her own.

She had begged her parents to let her ride. Full of hopes and dreams and aspirations of making the team one day, she had busted her ass to learn everything she could and spent countless hours on the ranch every day after school and most weekends. Her friends didn't understand her passion or devotion so it was a lonely journey but one that she treasured every single minute of.

Walking away from something she had loved so much almost killed her but so did the realization that she had lost everything that mattered most.

Now here they were, twenty-five years later, together again. Mike had dried many tears and had a world of advice back then. Nine years older than her, he had been like a big brother to her and she cherished him. Nine years didn't seem like a big deal now.

Mike set his coffee mug down on the table next to hers and pulled his chair around behind her. Rubbing and massaging her neck as they watched the sunrise rise up over the tree tops. He leaned closer to her and gently kissed her neck, knowing how it drove her crazy and he playfully worked his way his way around kissing the sensitive spot behind each ear.

"You are going to get in trouble if you keep that up," she teased, continuing to sip her coffee, enjoying the feeling of his affection. "I am so proud of you Mike. Did I ever tell you that?"

Sensing that Alexa really just wanted to enjoy the morning view together, Mike put his arms on her shoulders and massaged them instead of continuing to try to entice her to come back to bed as he had originally planned. He looked out over her shoulder at the view of all that he had built over the years and for the first time he understood why she enjoyed her morning ritual so much. Watching the sun glowing up over the tops of the barns, seeing the horses bathed in a fine mist of early morning fog was beautiful and peaceful. From this viewpoint, it was hard to believe that over all the years, he had never taken the time to see what his hard work and dedication had created. He had never seen it the way that she did. He had been too busy building it from the ground up to ever really see the broad view.

"It was never the same after you left."

"But look at what you created. People would give anything to have all of this. You have to be proud of what you have accomplished?"

"I don't know. In a way I am, but in another, I see all that it cost me in the process." Mike leaned back in his chair trying to appreciate the view that Alexa saw but to him that view was clouded by all of the things that he had lost and given up in his quest to chase his dreams at all cost. "A part of me changed that night in Reno. We had all thought we were invincible. That nothing could stop us from reaching our goals if we worked hard enough. I didn't know just how wrong I was until that night."

Alexa shivered at the mention of the accident, wrapping her arms tighter around herself she snuggled deeper inside the thick white waffle-textured robe she was wearing. That night had changed everything for all of them.

CHAPTER 13

"When they rushed you to the hospital in the ambulance I was terrified. I knew you were hurt but they weren't telling me anything. In the ER they wouldn't tell me what was going on either. I paced the hallways; stopping at the nurse's station every few minutes begging them to tell me how you were doing. I had thought the worst. That had been an ugly fall and even the paramedics were afraid of a neck injury as they carefully placed the neck brace on and strapped you to the backboard before carrying you to the ambulance."

Sitting across the desk from Mike, Alexa just quietly listened. They had never talked about the accident nor had she wanted to and until he had

brought it up this morning, she had never considered the sequence of events that unfolded from his
viewpoint. There were so many things about that
night that she had no memory of and so many
things that she wished she could forget.

"That night still haunts me like a bad dream
that just didn't seem real," Mike ran his fingers
through his hair as he recalled the events. "I blamed
myself and still do."

"The accident wasn't your fault Mike,"
Alexa replied, but Mike continued as if he hadn't
even heard her.

"At nineteen you were considered an adult.
They asked for your parent's contact information
but a few minutes later a nurse came out and said
that you didn't want anyone calling your parents.
When they rolled you out of the exam room towards surgery you were pretty out of it and a nurse
said I could wait in the waiting room and they
would let me know when you were in recovery."
Mike stood up out of his chair and walked over to
the window behind his desk, leaning one shoulder
against the window frame staring out of the glass.

Alexa could tell by his pause and his body language that he was fighting to keep his emotions in check.

"After what seemed like hours, the surgeon finally came out, assumed that I was family and told me that you had broken your collar bone, had several torn ligaments, a nasty lateral sprain on your right ankle, and had fractured your pelvic bone. The good news was that there were no permanent neck or spinal cord injuries. The surgery had gone well and he expected the bones to heal with no permanent damage. He had said the rest would just take time to heal."

"If they only knew just how wrong that prognosis had been," Alexa thought but didn't say a word.

"I was so relieved to hear him say that there were no spinal injuries. That had been all I could think about when I saw you hit the ground. The way you had landed — then, when you didn't try to get up or even move — I thought the worst. I froze. I couldn't move. I couldn't even move to get to you. It was Andre that got to you first."

Alexa shuddered as she listened to Mike fill in the missing pieces of that afternoon. The parts that she did remember, she had spent a lifetime trying to forget. She remembered hitting the ground, the sharp unbearable pain, and then it all went black.

"It wasn't until the next day that I found out about Gabri. They had you heavily sedated and I was not leaving you alone. I didn't know what to do — so I curled up in the chair next to your bed and just sat there, praying — praying for you to wake up and that it was all just a bad dream. I must have dozed off because the next thing I knew the nurse was tapping me on the shoulder. 'Sir, you really should go home and get some rest. We can call you in the morning when she wakes up.' I gave them my number, but they never called."

"I told them not to…" Alexa answered him.

Mike spun around from the window to face her, "Why would you do that? Why? I didn't understand then and I still don't understand now."

Alexa slid the locket side to side on the fine silver chain that hung around her neck the way she always did when she thought about that night, and the tears just silently started rolling down her cheeks.

"He had the tiniest little fingers and little toes... " she stammered, fighting to hold back the snobs, letting the tears roll down her face.

"Alexa what are you talking about?"

"I always lose everything that I love. Brent, Gabri, you, Andre, and ..." Alexa couldn't hold it in any longer and she let the pain and the tears flow as she curled herself into a ball, bringing her knees close to her chest and wrapping her arms tightly around them, burying her face in against her thighs trying to shield herself from the pain that threatened to drown her.

"Alexa what happened?" Mike rounded the corner of the large executive desk but her words stopped him from getting any closer.

"I didn't want anyone to know. Not you, not Andre, and damn sure not Brent," Alexa answered him, turning her pain into anger in an instant.

"What on God's earth are you talking about? You aren't making any sense."

"Let it go — Mike just let it go. Please..." Alexa wiped her eyes with the back of her hands as they both heard the sound of the backdoor shut and Andre's voice calling them from down the hall.

Alexa immediately straightened herself in the chair, planting both feet on the floor and then froze at the sound of Andre's voice.

"Hey, where are you two?" Andre called out, his voice echoing down the long hallway that led to Mike's private office.

Alexa barely had time to dry her eyes before Andre rounded the corner into the office.

Before Alexa could think, Andre had scooped her out of the chair and into his arms spinning her around.

"I heard you were in town. I didn't believe it and here you are, in the flesh. My God it's been so long. Where the hell have you been?"

"Put her down Andre."

Andre set her down on her feet and she took two steps backward before looking up.

"Alexa, what's wrong? Why are you crying?" When she didn't answer, Andre spun around in Mike's direction. "Mike what have you done?

Why is Alexa so upset that she looks like she has been drug behind a pick-up?"

"Me? What did I do? The hell if I know."

"Stop it. Both of you! Just stop it now! Neither one of you know the whole truth — so quit acting like assholes."

"It was Andre — I seduced him not the other way around," the words tumbling from her mouth before she could stop them. "I was so angry with Brent and so hurt. Out of sheer rebellion and a need to stop the pain, I set my sights on Andre because I knew it was the one thing that would even the score — or at least to me," Alexa continued without pausing or waiting for one of them to interject.

"I was four months pregnant when I took that spill in Reno…" Alexa couldn't tell who looked more shocked but she couldn't give a shit.

As Mike took a step forward she glared at him.

"You heard me." She threatened, stopping Mike in his tracks. "I was the one who initiated it. I was seething and hurt by Brent's betrayal. I stayed late at the arena practicing, trying to burn off the stress. Andre had already stabled his horse for the night and was getting ready to leave. I couldn't cool off and I was pushing my mare way past the point that I knew better. Andre didn't like the idea of me riding late at night alone — I guess he could tell by my mood that I damn sure needed to quit for the night so he turned around and climbed up on the arena rails and called out to me to ride over to where he was sitting."

Mike was standing in the middle of the room but didn't make a move in her direction, shocked and stunned by her anger and not wanting to believe what he was hearing. Andre leaned up against the corner of the desk, his hands gripping the edges of the desk behind him, remembering it all like it was yesterday.

CHAPTER 14

"Maybe you ought to give it a rest for to-night. Poor girl is slap worn out. You know Mike would throw a fit if he were here."

"Yes, but he is not!" Alexa snapped back.

"Whoa, take it easy."

"Why the hell should I?"

"Look Alexa, whatever is going on is not this mare's fault and you need to quit before one or both of you get hurt."

"Who do you think you are? You and Mike both…"

"Alexa we care about you. You have al-ways been like a sister to us and we give a shit what happens to you. Can you get that through your stubborn hot head?"

"Maybe I am sick and tired of being the little sister and having you two hounding me all the damn time."

Andre crossed the top rail and stepped into the arena snatching the reins with one hand. "That's enough. Get off. This mare has had enough and so have you."

"Get off now," reaching up with his right arm he encircled her waist pulling her down, letting her body slide against his until her feet touched the ground.

"I am not a kid anymore dammit!"

"Well you damn well are acting like one."

"That's really what you think?"

"Yes it is." Andre answered her as he walked the mare out of the arena and headed towards the alleyway.

"You insufferable smart ass!" Alexa stormed past him towards her private tack room. She could hear the distinctive sound of the mares iron shoes on the cement as Andre led her into the wash-rack. Hearing the sound of the water running as he rinsed the mare off before putting her up for the night only made it worse and Alexa threw her riding helmet onto one of the chairs and kicked the sand from her boots.

She knew she was wrong for working her mare so hard tonight and she felt bad. Inside she was still burning with the bitter rage of Brent's rejection. "To hell with him," she thought. "Two could play this game." Alexa unpinned her hair and bent over at the waist to shake the long natural curls loose, using her fingers to fluff the ends. She flipped her head back as she stood up and let them fall freely down her back. Her white sleeveless button-down shirt was wet from her feverish workout and was clinging to her skin. Undoing the buttons one at a time, stopping at the one just above the center of her bra, feeling the cool night air against her skin, a plan crossed her mind.

The last thing she wanted to do right then was to go home, alone. She could hear the sound of the metal sweat scraper as Andre scraped the water from the mare's back, neck, and sides.

The anger and resentment of Brent's rejection and the dismissal and reproach from Andre only fueled the fire burning deep inside of her. She needed the release. She needed to feel loved and wanted; and she needed to feel the emotional and physical high that only one thing could produce.

With the plan already forming in her head, Alexa turned out the light and closed the door of her tack room behind her. Entering the main alleyway, Alexa spotted Andre leading Gabri towards her stall. The stable hands would have already prepared the stalls before leaving for the night. They were alone in the barn which was rare. It was now or miss her chance. Alexa picked up her pace to intercept Andre as he was closing the stall door.

"Andre, wait! I want to apologize for taking my anger out on you. I never meant to say those things."

"But that is how you feel, isn't it?"

"Sometimes, yes. I feel like you and Mike treat me like a kid and I'm tired of feeling that way. I'm not a kid anymore Andre."

"How well I know it," Andre answered her, remembering the feeling of her body pressed against his as he had slid her down off of her mare. His body had instinctively reacted to each and every

curve. It was at that moment that he actually realized that she had grown up under their very eyes but
they hadn't been ready to admit it, even to themselves. He had noticed the way the grooms watched
her when they thought no one was paying attention,
careful to look away if either he or Mike was
around. When he had heard rumors of her and Brent
spending way too much time together he had tried
to warn her to leave him alone, knowing that Brent
didn't have a good intention in his brain. Brent was
an up and coming rider with a cocky attitude. She
deserved better.

"I don't know what all happened with you
and Brent and honestly it is none of my business but
I tried to warn you to stay away from him."

"Andre the last thing I need right now is a
lecture or 'I told you so'."

"I get it, but you deserve better than that."

"I know I do." Alexa lowered her eyes. The
distance between them was so close that she could
feel the warmth radiating from his body. She wanted to feel his arms engulf her. She wanted him to
hold her in his arms and make the world go away.
Lifting her chin up and meeting his gaze, Alexa

reached out to place her hand on his chest letting her fingers spread gently through the coarse masculine hair and loved the feeling of it beneath her fingertips. "Hold me Andre." Alexa let her hand slide ever so slowly down the deep crease between the muscles of his broad chest. She could feel the rise and fall of his chest as his breathing changed.

Andre brought his hands up to grip her shoulders, "Don't do this Alexa."

"Please Andre, just hold me." She continued to let her fingers drift even lower.

"Alexa you are right, you aren't a kid anymore and I can't keep pretending that you are." Andre continued to hold her at a safe distance but didn't retreat from her touch. "Alexa, I'm not Brent. I'm a grown man with needs of my own and I don't think you are in any way ready to handle that."

Alexa felt the sharp sting of his words and she closed her hand into a fist tangled in the mass of curly hairs, pulling herself even closer to him, wanting him to feel the same sharp pain that his words had caused. He hadn't even flinched but she felt him inhale so deeply that his entire chest seemed to expand to twice its size. She brought her other arm around to encircle his lower back and used the leverage that it gave her to close the space between them. Twisting loose from his grip, she stepped forward placing one long slender leg between his and leaned her head into his chest.

Alexa felt Andre's grip on her shoulders release as he let his arms lower around her waist and draw her into his body. She could feel the pressure of his hands on her lower back and she relaxed into his embrace. With her face resting on his chest she could feel his heart beating faster and when he gently kissed the top of her head something inside of her changed.

The feelings sweeping through her body were nothing like the feelings that Brent had aroused in her. This wasn't at all what she had planned or even imagined. With Brent there had been the hot burning sensation that electrified every nerve in her body, but there had also been the awkward feeling of friction between two separate bodies moving against each other. It had been raw and reckless, feeling more like a wrestling match as they each sought relief from the desire threatening to consume them.

In Andre's arms she felt as if she had melted into his body, their breathing synchronized, with a feeling of being one unit merging together. The feeling of his hands on her lower back spread a warmth through her that made her want to press even closer into his body. She could hear his heart pounding in her ear and she turned her face slightly to gently kiss his chest and inhale the very scent that was filling her with desire.

Through his jeans she could feel his desire hardening and rising between them as their hips pressed even closer to each other. Almost in a faint whisper she heard his voice, "Alexa we can't do this," but he made no move to release her from his embrace.

"Andre, please...please don't let go. I need you."

"Alexa you don't know what you are asking of me."

Tilting her head back to look him in the eyes she countered his hesitance, "Yes I do. I have never felt this safe, this loved, or this needed in my whole life. You were right. Brent just took what he wanted and ran. He never made me feel the way that I feel right this minute."

"You are so young and have so much to learn yet."

"So teach me."

"Alexa, we both know this is wrong. I'm not the right person — this isn't right."

"Would you rather see me with someone like Brent instead?" Alexa stiffened her whole body and stared up at him in defiance. "Would that make you happy to watch me get my heart ripped into a million pieces again?"

"Hell No! I would have ripped him into a million pieces — and should have."

"Then teach me what it is like to be really loved and cared for honestly and without pretenses. Teach me how it should be."

"Alexa this needs to stop."

"I dare you to deny that you don't feel it too," and she let her hand slide down past his waist, along the length of his jeans to caress the hard length that betrayed his denial.

Andre reached down and closed his hand around her wrist, "Alexa I am only human and if you don't stop what you're doing we are going to both regret it."

"No, no I won't regret one single minute of it. No matter what happens, I will always have the memory of what it felt like to be made love to by someone who cared for me as a person not an object."

Looking back now, Alexa knew those words had been spoken from her heart and she had meant them, every single one of them. Now it seemed like a cruel twist of fate, the school of hard knocks had thwarted her every attempt at happiness. To this very minute she didn't regret the blissful summer they had spent together. She had been happier than she had ever dreamed possible, right up until the moment the bright blue plus sign had appeared in the window of the pregnancy test. From that moment on, everything had spun out of control.

CHAPTER 15

"Why didn't you tell me?" Mike demanded.

"Because I didn't want anyone to know."

"Well did you think it would just go away?"

"Well I guess it did, didn't it," Alexa lost it.

"I am so sorry Alexa. I didn't mean it like that. I wasn't thinking — please forgive me. Please..."

"He was there for me when you weren't."

"I was competing."

"I know that.

Andre had taken that summer off from competition after retiring his beloved horse Mialonga. Andre always said that a rider only gets lucky enough to have a horse like Mia once in a lifetime. The others can never take their place. He had decided to retire Mia at her prime; she deserved that much after the eight years and dozens of Grand Prix championships that she had given him. He had several new and upcoming horses at various levels of training but he didn't feel that they were ready just yet. "And besides," he had said, "I just haven't clicked with the right one yet.

Trainers and riders in all competitive equestrian sports know that to keep competing they have to always have several mounts in their lineup to carry them through their career. It takes years and years of training to get a horse to the Grand Prix level and that doesn't start overnight. One tragic accident, one bad injury, and it can all be over.

No serious competitor would take the risk of losing their one and only mount without a backup. Owners of dressage horses are always seeking the top trainers and riders with the hopes of gaining a world champion, but just because an owner thinks that their horse is "the one", isn't always enough.

It takes the right combination to make a great team and like any relationship, the team members have to have the right chemistry and dynamics to make it work. Andre had that with Mialonga. Alexa had that with Gabri.

And she had had that with Mike and Andre; together they had made a great team. The accident in Reno had changed everything.

After the accident she couldn't face returning to the ranch. When they had finally discharged her from the hospital, Alexa had returned home briefly and then made the decision to move out to the east coast and pursue a career in marketing. She had thrown herself into her studies and refused to have anything to do with anything that reminded her of her past. Following graduation she had accepted a position with a major marketing firm that afforded her the opportunity to travel all over the world and she had climbed the corporate ladder with the determination of reaching the top ranks in record time. In that, she had succeeded.

Twenty-five years later, a random twist of fate had led her to a chance encounter with an old friend and fellow competitor at a convention in Seattle. Alexa had spotted Chris from across the room and her first instinct had been to run for the nearest exit and back to the safety of her hotel room. Before she could make a hasty retreat Chris had spotted her as well and quickly excused himself from the group that he had been talking with and headed straight in her direction.

"Alexa, I can't believe it's you. How have you been?" Chris reached out to shake her hand. "I kind of figured you might be here. Seems you have made quite a name for yourself and your reputation as a brilliant and a formidable competitor in the marketing world is a well-known topic of conversation." Chris grinned. "I shouldn't be surprised; you always were, even when we were competing against each other in the show ring. I couldn't believe when I heard that you had quit riding."

"It was time move on and think about my future," Alexa answered him, trying to find a way to politely end the conversation.

"I ran into Mike not long ago and I asked him if he had heard from you."

At the mere mention of Mike's name, Alexa's demeanor changed. "Chris it was very nice running into you but I promised to meet with some clients and I am running behind schedule," Alexa stated, pretending to glance at her watch. "It was really nice to see you." And with that, Alexa excused herself and made a hasty retreat for the nearest exit.

Left standing there, Chris watched Alexa make her way across the room. "Damn. What a power-house. She sure turned out to be one hell of a woman," Chris thought to himself as he pulled his cell phone from his jacket pocket. He couldn't wait to tell Mike who he had just had the pleasure of running into and he fired off a quick text to Mike's cell number.

Before he could return the phone to his pocket it rang.

"Chris, don't play games with me. Are you telling me that Alexa is there?"

"Yep, in the flesh and looking hot as hell too!"

"Cut the shit Chris and get me her cell phone number. I want to talk to her."

"That won't be a problem. She is one of the keynote speakers this weekend."

"Get me her number."

"Will do. Getting her number is easy; getting her to talk to you might be a different situation. She didn't seem very happy when I brought your name up."

"Just get her number and don't mention that you spoke to me."

"No problem. And by the way, good luck. You are going to need it. She is one tough cookie in this business."

"Let me worry about that — thanks for calling — I owe you one."

As they ended their conversation Chris headed back to the group, knowing exactly which one of them most likely had access to Alexa's personal cell phone number. It didn't take long before he had the number in his phone and forwarded it on to Mike.

Riding through one of the brood mare pastures, miles out from the main areas of the ranch, Mike had stopped the truck when the call from Chris had interrupted him out of the blue. It was a phone call that he never had expected. He had tried many times to get in touch with Alexa over the years but had never been able to reach her. Her parents had both passed away and after that he had lost all contact with her. Running into Chris at a show in Pasadena had been a fluke. Neither Mike nor Chris was actively competing anymore but occasionally they were invited to perform clinics or exhibitions at different events. Mike usually politely declined the invitations, preferring to concentrate his time on the ranch operations rather than being actively involved in riding anymore. His breeding program took up much of his time and he liked it that way. Breeding and raising some of the world's best dressage bloodlines kept him challenged.

Andre had long ago taken over the training side of the operation along with several new trainers and it freed Mike to concentrate on the breeding operation instead. They had just recently sold two four-year olds to a group of owners in Europe. After Mike finalized the sale and handled the paperwork, Andre arranged for the transport and shipping, handling all of the arrangements with the new owners. Andre had also agreed to accompany the animals and spend a year or two working with the new trainers and riders to get the horses well on their way.

Unlike Mike, Andre had never married. Andre seemed to prefer to be alone and he lived and breathed for this sport. He had dedicated his entire life to it and Mike had always wondered why Andre had never even considered a long-term relationship in all the years that they had known each other. After Mike's second divorce, he had made Andre part owner in the business with a 60/40 % split between them with Andre also being his sole beneficiary. Neither one of them had heirs to inherit the ranch and Mike wanted to make sure that if anything ever happened to him that Andre would take full control of the operation and continue the dream that they had both worked so hard to build.

With Chris' phone call stirring his mind, Mike sat in the cab of the truck thinking about the past and how it had all begun, and how it had all changed. Things were very different after the accident in Reno. Andre had changed. Hell, they both had. They had lost more than just a teammate; they had lost a best friend. Sure, they had given her hell over the years but Mike had never expected her to just walk away and never look back. He had never understood her reasons.

Now, for the first time since that day, he could feel her presence like a ghost haunting his waking dreams and he stared at his phone impatiently waiting for the one thing that might bring her back. He just wanted to hear her voice again. Maybe, with some miracle of chance, he could convince her to come back even if it was just once.

CHAPTER 16

Chris had come through on his promise and Mike stared down at his phone not quite believing the text message giving him Alexa's contact information. "Now what?" Mike thought to himself. He had no idea what he intended to do with it. He stored the contact formation into his contacts list, put the phone in the console, started the truck, and headed back towards the barns. He would figure it out when he could clear his mind and think straight.

Later that night, sitting in his office, Mike had actually pulled up her number at least a dozen times, but changed his mind before tapping the call button. A text message out of the clear blue was too impersonal and besides, he wanted to hear her voice. Never one to be at a loss for words, this time he was. He had no clue what to say after so many years. Everything that came to his mind sounded wrong.

Mike leaned back into his leather desk chair and tried to think. After tossing countless ideas around in his head, Mike reached for his phone. "To hell with this — just call already," he told himself. Pulling up her number, he hit the green call button and heard the number start to ring. Each ring caused his pulse to race faster and faster with anticipation, then he heard it connect and the sound of her voice filled his ear.

"Hi, you've reached the voicemail of Alexa Connor. Sorry that I can't take your call right now, but please leave a message and I will return your call as soon as I am available." Mike didn't wait for the beep and instead hit the end call button and tossed the phone back onto his desk. "Dammit!"

He waited all of ten minutes before grabbing the phone and pressing the call button again. After several rings, the call went to her voicemail again. Just hearing the sound of her voice made him

more and more restless and he hung up without saying a word. She would see the missed calls. He
didn't want to leave a message. He couldn't even
think of what to say if she had answered but leaving
a message and having her not return the call was
more than he could bear at the moment. She had
refused to take any of his calls after they had returned from Reno and it had felt like a knife in his
chest each time.

Somehow he was hoping that time had
healed the old wounds but as he stared at the silent
phone on his desk he had his doubts.

Several times throughout the day and into
the evening, Mike had dialed her number only to
get her voicemail each time. It became increasingly
obvious that she had no intention of answering his
call nor had she tried to return his call either. He
hadn't left a message so why would she, Mike chid-
ed himself. "Now what?"

Mike had finished up for the day, taken a
hot shower and was stretched out in his recliner
flipping through the channels trying to get his mind
off of the sound of her voice that filled his head like
a song you can't stop hearing once it gets stuck in

your brain. It had been so many years since he had heard her voice; the sound of it was a much more mature and sophisticated version of what he remembered and at the same time it was just as familiar. Alexa's voice had always belied her actual small petite stature, especially if she was irritated or excited. Her voice had a deep resonance to it that carried her words further than imaginable. Yet it had a deep, sexy, sultry tone that could turn heads in an instant.

Mike decided to give it one more try before turning in for the night. Pulling up her number he took a deep breath before tapping the call button. Three rings and he heard the call switch to her voicemail, "Dammit Alexa, answer your damn phone!" Mike cursed to himself. Caught off-guard, he heard the beep alerting him that the voicemail was now in record mode. This time he didn't end the call, "Alexa, it's Mike. Please give me a call. I just want to say hello, Chris Latham gave me your cell number — I just want to hear your voice. Or just a text message letting me know how you are doing…" Mike ran out of words and ended the call.

It had been two weeks since he had left the message on her voicemail and Mike had given up, realizing that she had no intention of returning his call. He wouldn't try again. Whatever her reasons were, he couldn't handle the stone cold wall that she had built between them and he lost any hope that things might have changed over time.

Mike blocked it out of his mind and buried himself in the day-to-day business of running the ranch, filling up every minute of his free time knee-deep in the constant paperwork and research necessary to track and improve the current bloodlines that he was developing. He left no time to allow his mind to drift back to the past.

The fall weather was beginning to creep up on them bringing the cool, crisp morning breezes that signaled the changing season. This would be the last breeding season for the year and Mike was out in the breeding barns checking for heat cycles on the mares that he had selected to breed to one of his best stallions. The handlers had already gone through the morning ritual of teasing the mares by walking the stud horse through the long alleyway. He had a dedicated and well-trained crew that were all quite capable of handling the entire breeding process without his assistance but when it came to some of his prize bloodlines, he preferred to check the mares himself. Timing was crucial especially at this time of year in order to increase the conception rate. He had a lot riding on this particular breeding project. This was a high-dollar project with each cross designed to produce some excellent progeny with the potential for several top-level future mounts. He had a lot at stake with this round of breeding and he wanted to personally oversee the breeding process first hand.

Mike had just snapped the lead rope onto the halter of a mare that he had determined was at the peak of her heat cycle and was leading her out of her stall when his phone rang. With his mind occupied giving orders to the handlers, Mike reached into his jacket pocket and answered the call, "Mike Landon…"

"Mike, it's Alexa."

Stunned, Mike came to an immediate standstill, passing the lead rope to one of the handlers and motioning them to go on without him. "Alexa, is it really you?" Mike leaned up against the wooden stall door to steady himself from the flood of emotions that had suddenly made his legs feel incapable of supporting the rest of his body.

"Yes..." Alexa's voice paused before continuing. "Yes it is me."

"I don't even know what to say. Just hearing your voice..."

"I know the feeling. Hearing your voice on my voicemail shocked me too."

"There are a million things I want to say and ask, all jumbled up at once and I'm afraid that anything I say will have you vanish into thin air like an early morning dream."

"How's the ranch?" Alexa skirted the direction the conversation was heading before he could finish.

Letting her set the pace, Mike headed for safer emotional ground and answered, "The ranch is doing great. In fact I was in the middle of checking heats and bringing the first mare of the day to the breeding chutes when you called."

"If it is a bad time, I can let you go."

"No. Please don't hang up Alexa. The handlers can wait. It can all wait. The only thing I want to do right now is to talk to you."

Over the course of the following weeks they had slowly rebuilt a rapport to the point where they were calling and texting each other several times a day. He had worked so hard to convince Alexa to come back to the ranch. Getting her to trust him again had been a challenge. He had honestly thought that the past two years had put the past behind them and he had been seriously contemplating asking her to marry him. He hadn't wanted to overwhelm her but every time that she had to leave to fly out, his heart went into panic mode at the thought of her leaving again and never returning. He wanted her here on the ranch by his side for the rest of eternity and he had been so close to making that dream a reality but with two failed marriages behind him, it had kept him from really letting her know how much she meant to him.

Now he had shot it all to hell and back.

CHAPTER 17

Alexa hadn't seen Andre since the day of the blow-up in Mike's office. He had left the next morning for an event with some of the older riders. He had taken over much of the coaching and training since returning from Europe. From the balcony she had watched the trucks and trailers pulling out from the barns.

Things between her and Mike had been strained to say the least and the tension was almost unbearable at times. When Andre had found out that Mike had brought her to the club he had stormed out of the office slamming the door behind him and had avoided them both unless he had specific business to deal with, even then he was short and to the point.

Alexa had enough and it was time to cut through the tension if there was any hope of saving their relationship. Leaving the peace and quiet of the terrace she headed to Mike's office.

"This is my life Alexa; this is what makes me happy. Others cheat on their spouses and go to church on Sunday with a clear conscious. I am sick of that. Been there, done that, have the divorce papers to prove it. These couples live their lives without the shame and guilt. They are happy. I have waited my entire life for someone like you to share my world with. Two failed marriages and countless relationships that always ended with me walking away. My first wife couldn't handle me being gone from home while I was competing. The jealousy, anger and resentment became so great that I didn't even want to go home anymore."

"Once I retired from competition, my second wife couldn't handle the long hours and dedication that it took to build and operate the equestrian center or the ranch. She was actually jealous of the time I spent with my students and it was downhill from there. After that marriage ended I was convinced that a happy marriage was not for me. Maybe some people are just not cut out to be monogamous."

Alexa didn't say a word. She just let him vent. She had pushed his buttons first by barging into his office intent on working out their differences and instead it had only irritated him more.

"Hell Alexa, I didn't cheat on my wives because I didn't love them. I just needed more. Everything would be great for the first few months or even years then we would slowly drift apart and I would start feeling smothered. The bickering, fighting, petty jealousy and constant interrogation every night would drive me up the wall until I just didn't want to go home. I didn't want to walk in the door and feel like a kid sent to the principal's office."

Mike paused for a moment and when Alexa didn't say anything, he continued his rant. She had hit a raw nerve and it wouldn't be ignored.

"This sport, this ranch is my life. It isn't a 9 to 5 job. It is 24/7. You know that. I retired at the top of my career because I thought that being home would save my relationship but it only made things worse."

Alexa sat quietly, letting him vent. She wanted him to blow off the tension so that they could try to resolve the issues that had pulled them apart. "I understand Mike."

"When I was competing and traveling constantly, at least she actually missed me — or at least pretended to. We would have wild, passionate sex like two teenagers in love for the first time. After we had burned off the aching need then we would make love and cuddle together wrapped in each other's arm. I needed that! I needed the excitement — the thrill— the rush — and the emotional bonding."

Alexa just nodded her head, listening intently as he shared his own personal feelings with her. She knew he needed to vent. Instead of feeling jealous hearing him talk about his past relationships, she felt empathy, knowing all too well exactly what he was expressing. Her own marriage had been a wreck and for many of the same reasons.

She had craved the romance and exploration of new and exciting things. For her ex-husband, sex was just a bodily function that revolved solely around his needs only.

Alexa had never actually cheated on her husband — she wanted to — she thought about it, and even swore to herself that she would. Ultimately it would always come down to her unwillingness to break the vows that she had made the day they married, when she made a promise she kept it. To go back on her word was something she refused to do.

If she had never known the powerful and intoxicating pleasure of mind-blowing orgasms, maybe she could have been happy. You don't miss what you never had.

CHAPTER 18

"So you mean to tell me that after introducing me to your lifestyle, meeting and making friends with other couples that profess that it makes their relationship stronger not weaker, that you believe in that concept?"

"Yes. I do believe that — whole-heartedly."

"Then why do you have a problem excepting the love that Andre and I have for each other?"

"Because — that is totally different."

"How is it different?"

"It just is!"

"No it isn't! I love Andre in one way and I love you in a different way. But I am in love with both of you."

"How did the two of you manage to keep your relationship a secret? And Why?"

"Neither one of us wanted anyone to know — especially you."

"Smart move on your part because I would have choked the life out of him if I had known. "

"It was none of your business."

"None of my business…"

"Yes, it was none of your business. Andre tried his best to dissuade me but I was hell bent on erasing Brent's memory.

"He sure as hell didn't try hard enough!"

"I just tried harder. I needed him! I needed to feel loved again — to feel safe."

"I'm not buying it. He knew better."

"It just happened. Can't you just accept that?"

"No! No I can't."

"Well I don't think you have a choice."

"Oh I have a choice, and right now I don't think you would like it very much."

"So that's how it is? You and only you? My feelings don't matter."

"Not when it comes to Andre. That, I can't handle."

"You two-faced son of a bitch."

"Alexa, be real. You can't expect me to accept the fact that you are still in love with Andre — after all these years. After the last two years that we have been together? What was that Alexa? Some game you were playing — using me to have a chance to be with Andre again?"

"It isn't like that at all."

"Then what is it?"

"I never expected to have my past drug up and thrown in my face. I thought the past was the past — I spent years running away from all of it. I never expected it all to come flying back like it was yesterday."

"What's up with the locket Alexa? I have noticed it from the first day you came back —how you hold it or slide it around — especially when you are quiet or nervous. Who gave it to you? Did Andre?"

"No," Alexa's voice changed and she instinctively reached for the locket as she felt the tears well up in her eyes. "I bought it for myself to keep him with me."

"Who? Andre?"

"Things were different back then — not like it is now. They didn't even want to let me see him. But there was this one nurse. She had lost a baby and knew what I was going through so she made them wait while she cleaned him — she brought him to me so I could see him. She stamped his tiny foot prints on a card." The tears just rolled down her cheeks as Alexa remembered each and every tiny detail about him.

Mike pulled her into his chest and held onto her for dear life. "I am so sorry Alexa," he said, gently rubbing her back. "Why didn't you tell me? Why did you face that kind of pain alone? I was right there — pacing the floors — waiting and wanting to be with you."

"But it was Andre that I needed. I needed to see him — I wanted him to be there."

"If I had only known, I swear Alexa. I would have moved the world that night or done anything not to see you suffer." Mike held her until there were no more tears left and wiped her face with his hands. "Can I see it?"

Alexa stepped back slightly and placed the silver locket in his hands. She watched him as his finger stroked the silver lid engraved with a tiny angel. She watched him turn it over to read the inscription engraved on the back that simply read... "Tyler," with the date of the accident engraved below it.

Alexa flinched as Mike clicked the latch to open the locket. She watched him as he stared down at the two tiny foot prints and for the first time since she had known him, she saw the tears well up in his eyes as he gently closed the locket.

CHAPTER 19

"Andre I have to go. I don't belong here anymore." Andre had read the text message in disbelief. He was on his way back to the ranch from the show and was still about an hour away from the ranch. He had frantically dialed her number a dozen times with no answer. He was already doing well over the speed limit and pulling the 40-foot, gooseneck trailer loaded with six horses required all of his concentration. Trent was having a hell of time keeping up with him and had called him several times throwing a fit. Trent was behind him pulling the 34-foot trailer with four horses and three of the younger riders.

Andre eased back on the accelerator to let Trent catch-up. He had all of their lives at stake and being reckless wasn't going to solve anything. Andre consoled himself with the hope that Mike would not let her leave this time and tried to keep his focus on the road.

Andre stormed into Mike's office after hearing that Alexa had in fact packed her things and headed to the airport. One of the stable hands had told him that he had seen her rental car heading down the long driveway towards the front gates.

"Mike, are you really going to let her leave? After all these years you are going to just let her walk out and disappear again?"

"Andre she needs time to sort out her own feelings."

"To hell with that. You let her leave once and walk out of both of our lives — without so much as a good-bye!"

"Andre I am telling you, leave it be."

"No. You wouldn't let me see her the night of the accident — I should have been there. Fuck this…"

"Look Andre, her mind is so mixed up right now that the only thing you are going to do is hurt her more."

"No, dammit. You already did that."

"We both did and if I could take it all back I would — in a second — but I can't."

"Well if you won't stop her, I damn sure will. I am not letting her leave here like the last time. I may have been an idiot back then to think the pain would go away; that I wouldn't miss her; that I didn't lover her. I learned that lesson the hard way. And then to find out that she has been back here for the last two years and you never said a damn word."

"How does that make you feel now Andre? Knowing she has been back and had not even tried to contact you?"

"Fuck you Mike."

"How do you think I felt after founding out everything?"

"I didn't know about the baby. After the accident it was you sitting by her bedside. When the vet told me that Gabri had suffered irreparable damage to both front legs and shoulder muscles and wouldn't be able to make the trip back to Denver — I was the one that had to make the decision and sign the papers to have her put down. I knew that it was going to tear Alexa's heart in two and she would hate me for it."

"You made the right call when it came to Gabri. I would have done the same thing and so would have Alexa. She would never have let Gabri suffer. You know that."

"I wanted to see her. I wanted to be at the hospital by her side. And now — finding out about the baby — I hate myself even more because I wasn't there for her. I didn't have a clue. I had to get all of the gear and the horses loaded and head back to the ranch. No one knew what was going on — how bad Alexa was injured. Everyone was asking me and I didn't have the answers. I didn't hear anything from you until the next morning. Why didn't you call me? You knew we were all worried sick!"

"Alexa was my only concern that night. I knew and trusted you to handle things on that end. Hell they weren't telling me anything — Alexa was in and out of it — too upset to even speak to me.

She didn't even want me there — she refused to let me call her parents. It wasn't until four o'clock in the morning that I made it back to my hotel room, tried to rest, but I couldn't sleep. I stared at the phone waiting for it to ring like the nurses had promised. But it never did."

"Why didn't you call me?"

"It was too early in the morning and I didn't want to tie up the phone in case they tried to reach me. As the hours drug on I finally did call and when I heard the news about Gabri it tore my heart out. How was I going to tell her that?"

"You should have let me see her. Maybe things would have been different. Maybe she would have told me about the miscarriage. I can understand her not wanting you to know but I would like to think that she would have told me — I should have been there."

"I knew nothing about it and obviously she had her reasons for not telling you before. I don't understand any of it."

"Did she ask to see me? I have to know."

"She didn't want to see anyone. Looking back the only odd clue that I apparently missed back then because I wasn't even thinking straight, was when the surgeon had said, '*The rest would take time.*' That had to be what he was talking about and assumed I knew what he meant."

"She never talked about it?"

"Not a word. She didn't even want me around, but I stayed. I was not leaving her in the hospital alone. She barely spoke and they had her so sedated due to the severity of the injuries. The nurses would ask me to leave the room when they needed to check on her. I would sit out in the waiting room dozing on and off.

"I am still furious that you wouldn't let me up there to see her before I had to leave."

"I didn't see a reason for it — you had your hands full with the horses. I would go to the hotel, take a shower, get something to eat and head back to the hospital. I had the hotel staff move her things into my room because I had no idea how long she would be in the hospital. I did call her parents and kept them informed but I knew they couldn't make the trip up there. I promised them that I would stay with her whether she liked it or not. I wasn't leaving."

"But you made me leave without seeing her."

"Now that I know the whole story, I am sorry that I did."

"Well I am not letting her leave again…whether you like it or not," Andre said as he slammed the door.

Trent and the crew already had the horses unloaded by the time that Andre made it back to the stable. "Unhook the goose-neck Trent — I need my tuck!'' Andre had the truck running before Trent could disengage the fifth-wheel hitch from the bed of the truck.

"Where are you going?" Trent called out to Andre as he jumped down from the bed of the truck and made sure the landing leg was locked down before Andre pulled the truck away from the trailer.

Andre whipped the truck around in front of the main stable and headed back towards the front gates, stopping long enough to answer Trent and give him orders to unload the tack and have the trailers cleaned. "I have to get to the airport — just handle it until I get back."

Andre had already wasted precious time confronting Mike when he should have just left for the airport immediately when he heard the news. The airport was two hours away and he had no idea what flight she was on or what time it was scheduled to depart. Without the weight of the trailer and barring any traffic, he might be lucky to cut thirty or forty minutes off of the trip; parking would be the nightmare. If she had scheduled a last minute flight he might be lucky to catch her in time. And if he didn't, he would be on the next plane out if he had to, Mike might be an idiot, but Andre refused to let her leave without a damn good reason. Running away had not solved anything in the past and it wasn't going to solve things now.

Turning out of the gates, Andre floored the one-ton and hit the highway heading towards the interstate. His phone was still in the console connected to the charger but he didn't have time to waste trying to type and drive. Besides, he didn't want her to know he was on the way. Knowing Alexa she would panic and get on an even earlier flight if she knew. She could be so damn stubborn and hardheaded when she had her mind made up. She had avoided them all for twenty-five years.

When Andre had returned from Europe he had settled back into his house and into his routine at the training center. Owen and Trent had kept things running smoothly in his absence. It was during one of their first meetings, days after his return that Trent had brought up the news about Mike's latest relationship. Mike's relationships were always hot topics of gossip because he never kept one around longer than a couple of months. After Mike's second divorce, he had espoused a lifestyle that Andre just could not come to terms with, to each his own, but Andre had lost interest in Mike's string of affairs a long time ago.

But it was something that Trent had said that had him curious enough to dig in deeper. According to Trent, Mike had been seeing the same one for almost two years. Seems she would fly in, spend the weekends several times a month and fly back out on Mondays. Sometimes staying for a week or two but it wasn't the norm. Questioning Trent further, Andre learned that she was some hot-shot executive and had a way of keeping Mike in line. Trent had joked about that part.

"She is a little bitty might of a thing," Trent had joked. "Good looking and sassy but not very friendly — but she sure keeps Mike walking tall," Trent had grinned at his own joke.

Something about Trent's rambling caught Andre's attention. This didn't sound like any of Mike's normal tall, long legged blondes that Mike normally preferred. "Does she ride?" Andre had questioned.

"Nanh, she rarely comes in the stables and when she does she just hangs out and watches. Never spoken to her myself."

"Wonder how he managed to keep this one, this long?" Andre had joked back.

"That's what we all have been trying to figure out. She stayed up at the guest house the first four or five times. Didn't take Mike long to convince her otherwise," Trent grinned.

"And she wasn't a client?" Andre had asked.

"Not as far as we know."

"That's odd, even for Mike."

"That's what we thought too," Trent replied.

"What does she look like?" Andre questioned Trent further. Something in his gut told him that Mike's latest romance was no stranger and his heart began to beat faster.

"Like I said, she is not much more than five-feet tall, long reddish brown wavy hair — can't weigh more than a feather — but she definitely has all the right curves, in all the right places. Sexy in her own sort of way, just not the bombshell, plastic type Mike usually has draped on his arm." Trent stated.

"And she doesn't ride?" Andre asked again.

"Not that I have ever seen." Trent answered.

"When was the last time she was here?"

"A couple weeks ago, I think."

Andre had a very strong feeling that he knew exactly who she was and one phone call to Maria had confirmed it. Alexa was back. At first he had been mad as hell knowing what Trent had told him, that she and Mike had been involved in a relationship for the past two years. It burned his ass up knowing that fact.

The last time he had seen her was when the paramedics had loaded her into the back of the waiting ambulance. He had been the first one at her side when her mare had spooked and reared up, tossing Alexa into the air. She had hit the ground so hard that it had knocked her helmet loose as she rolled twice before landing on her back motionless. She had looked like a ragdoll lying in the dust. Andre had cleared the rails and been at her side in an instant. He immediately felt for a pulse. He had placed his ear next to her mouth. She was unconscious, but still breathing. The paramedics had arrived right behind him and taken charge. Andre remembered just standing there, watching them work and being terrified.

Mike had finally made his way through the crowd and gripped him on his shoulder. Together they had just watched and waited for any sign that she would come to and say something. Once she was securely strapped to the backboard, Andre and Mike had both helped the two paramedics carry her to the ambulance. The last image he had of her was as they closed the rear doors and raced away with lights and sirens. Mike had insisted on following the ambulance to the hospital, giving Andre orders to take care of getting everything together.

When he returned to the arena he could see the veterinarians working on Gabri. The mare had been the last thing on his mind until Alexa had been loaded into the ambulance. Now he had to focus his attention on her mare. He could see her repeatedly trying to get to her feet and fighting the handlers. The vets had no choice but to sedate her in order to safely remove her from the arena.

After several hours, the vets had done all they could and it was clear that the mare was not going to make it through the ordeal. His brain was in a fog as they explained the injuries and asked him to sign the papers to have her humanely put down or whether he wanted to wait to consult Mike. As he had signed his name on the forms, his heart felt like it would explode in his chest. The images of the mare trying to regain her footing; the sight of Alexa lying motionless in the arena — the sight of the mare going over backwards — the sight of Alexa tumbling through the air — the gasping sounds of the crowd — the lights, the sirens wailing — it was all too much. It was like a horrible movie flashing through his mind over and over. Those were the last images he had of her.

Finding out that she had finally returned to the ranch after all these years, just made him want to see her, see her walking and talking and smiling like she had before that night. Nothing else mattered.

Over the years he had wanted to contact her but never did. He had heard that she had married an attorney a few years after graduating from college but it hadn't lasted. And as far as he knew, she had never returned to the sport that she had once lived and dreamed for.

He had told himself that having her back at the ranch, even if she was now with Mike, was better than the years he had spent without her. Seeing her in Mike's office that first day, knowing it was really her, had seemed like all of his prayers had finally been answered. She was back.

Now if he didn't make it to the airport in time, she would be gone again. That wasn't something he was willing to accept — not this time —

not ever. Not now that he knew everything. Andre floored the accelerator and switched lanes, swerving around slower moving vehicles. He had to make it to the airport before she could leave.

CHAPTER 20

N ever in her wildest dreams would Alexa have believed the strange twist of fate that had brought both Mike and Andre back into her life, especially in the context of their current relationship. When Mike first introduced her to the open lifestyle that had become part of his world, she had been confused, unsure, and extremely apprehensive about the whole concept. She had not even thought it conceivable to love two people so equally and yet so differently.

Deep in her heart she truly believed that her feelings for Andre were long ago buried in the past. She had spent years running from that past and thought that she had finally healed the hole left in her heart. She had grown up and chalked up the mistakes of her youth to lessons learned and nothing more. Denial has a way of doing that.

But seeing Andre again and having Mike drag up the past just opened a floodgate of emotions that she had not been prepared to deal with at all. With the three of them back together again she could no longer run from the pain or bury it in the past. She loved them both and Mike's ultimatum to choose only made her realize that leaving them both was her only option. Choosing one over the other was something her heart wouldn't allow her to do.

The first night at the club, she hadn't given Leza's words much thought when Leza had explained that many of the people there were threesomes by choice. That had just been such a foreign concept to her, too foreign to even process. Now she understood what Leza had been trying to tell her. Maybe that lifestyle wasn't for everyone but for some, it was the only one that allowed them to be truly happy. Being able to share her life with the two people she loved the most without having to choose one over the other was going to be a challenge. So many self-professed monogamous couples actually have a spouse at home and cheat behind their back. What makes them right in thinking that is a perfect situation?

Mike had introduced her into a world where consensual non-monogamy between consenting adults was a better alternative to the lying and cheating that many couples go through. But ultimately, when it came down to actually accepting her love and need to have Andre back in her life, Mike had flipped. His own beliefs had been challenged.

Torn between the two of them, Alexa knew that she could never choose and walking away from them both had seemed like the only solution. Leaving the ranch and the past behind, just as she had done the first time was all she had on her mind.

Sitting in the airport terminal, surrounded by strangers, she felt her heart shattering into a million pieces all over again. She tried texting message after message but deleted each one without sending them. There were no words left to say that would make any of it right, nor ease the pain welling up inside of her. As she heard the boarding call being announced, she put her phone on vibrate, gathered up her things and headed towards the line forming at the gate. She had already opened the electronic boarding pass and was waiting for her turn to scan the image on her phone when it vibrated in her hand. Turning the phone over to make sure that the boarding pass was still on the screen, she saw the text from Andre.

"Alexa, don't you dare get on that plane! Don't you run away again, I mean it!"

She read the message and panic made her step out of the line as she re-read the message again. The line of passengers continued to move through the check-in terminal as she stayed rooted in her tracks unable to process her next move. The phone went off again and she read the message.

"I can't get through security, but for God's sake please don't leave. If you don't answer this message, I will be on the next plane out of here, but you aren't running away again!"

Alexa stared up from her phone as she heard the woman at the gate address her, "Ma'am, will you be boarding this flight?" Alexa felt like she was caught in a time warp as she looked down the gangway as the last of the passengers were already boarding and she stared back down at her phone in disbelief.

"Ma'am, if you are boarding this flight you need to do so now before we close the gate."

"I have to go…" Alexa answered her as she took off down the concourse towards the security area.

Andre was already in line at the ticket counter when he heard Alexa's voice, "Andre, wait!" He felt his pulse racing as he rushed to meet her halfway. Alexa dropped her bags as Andre picked her up off of her feet and hugged her so tight that she thought she would lose her breathe just as he covered her mouth with his, breathing life back into her soul.

Andre wiped away the tears rolling down her face, pressed his lips to her forehead and said, "Don't worry, we will figure it all out. Let's just get you home where you belong."

He hugged her one last time, picked up her bags with one hand as he wrapped his other arm around her waist and escorted her out of the airport.

After getting Alexa settled in the passenger seat, Andre opened the rear door of the pick-up, placed her bags on the seat and pulled his phone from his pocket to fire off a quick text to Mike.

"I have her and we are on our way back." Andre put the phone back in his pocket, closed the door and went around to the driver's side not waiting for a response.

As Andre eased the truck out of the parking garage he couldn't help but notice how visibly shaken Alexa was, as she sat motionless and quiet, staring straight ahead with her hands tightly hugging her shoulders. Andre knew her well enough to know that her mind was going a hundred miles a minute but that she had closed herself off to any outside intrusion. Talking wasn't what she needed or wanted at that moment so he turned the radio on and gave her the freedom to be alone with her own thoughts while he focused on navigating through the rush hour traffic.

CHAPTER 21

Mike was pacing the length of the alleyway trying to concentrate on checking that the horses had all been put away before the stable hands had left for the evening, but his phone was burning a hole in his pocket as he waited each second for it to ring. He had re-read Andre's last text a dozen times and the minutes seemed like hours. Somewhere in the back of his mind he realized how excruciating it must have been for Andre all those years ago when he had been waiting every second to hear anything about how Alexa was doing. It pained him to think how he hadn't taken the time to call Andre back then and how sorry he was all these years later.

Knowing that even without traffic it would still take Andre at least two hours to make it back to the ranch; Mike decided to head back to the main house. Hoping that tackling the mound of paperwork on his desk would help pass the time but doubting even his own idea of such a solution. Alexa was the only thing on his mind. She had been up since before dawn and packed without even grabbing a cup of coffee much less anything to eat. She had to be starving and exhausted which only made him worry even more.

He had not realized that she had packed and left until Andre had busted into his office with the news. It was always Alexa's habit of getting up before daybreak and sitting out on the terrace with her coffee and breakfast. She always let him sleep in, preferring her quiet solitude in the early morning. She would eventually come back to bed and snuggle in as he was just waking up, always ready for a playful round of lovemaking to officially start the day. She could be a handful but he loved every minute of it. It brought a smile to his face just thinking about it.

But now he was worried. He had let his damn pride cause him to do and say things that he couldn't take back. Maybe she was right. Maybe Andre knew and understood her better than he thought he had. Andre brought out a different side of her personality. Together they were different in a way he had never really noticed before. With Andre she was calmer, quieter and more settled. It was almost peaceful to watch the way they worked together as a team in everything they did. Perhaps that was the reason that he had never even had a clue of their relationship back then. They had seemed like best friends that were inseparable. He had been too busy with running the ranch and competing to take much notice.

Sitting behind his desk in his private office he continuously stared up at the clock watching the minutes creep by, glancing at his phone willing it to ring. Andre had promised to come straight to the ranch after picking Alexa up. He gazed upwards and said a silent prayer of thanks that Andre had stopped her before she had boarded the plane. He knew firsthand how stubborn she could be when her mind was made up. He had always challenged her and she never backed down or gave in and always pushed herself to the limit to please him. She was feisty, quick-witted and stubborn at times but she never quit trying.

Maybe that was the difference between their relationships. She had said it herself the night he had made his ultimatum and demanded that she choose between the two of them. She had refused and quickly flipped the coin and challenged his beliefs. He had spent years embracing the open lifestyle concept. In his mind, it afforded him everything that he needed. It was a world where people could be totally free to explore their own sexuality without the taboos and stigmas. Couples loved each other deeply and honestly. They didn't have a need to hide or lie or cheat behind their partners backs, unlike so many monogamous couples. He had really believed that and embraced it, until Alexa had challenged him, igniting in him a possessive need to have her as his own.

He had never had a clue that she and Andre had been involved in a relationship that went far deeper than the close bond as friends. Not until everything had been drug out into the open, did he ever imagine that the two of them had been involved in their own love affair. When Alexa had come back, Andre had been in Europe and she never once asked about him or even talked about the past. She had pretty much avoided the barns and horses altogether. He had assumed the memories were just too painful for her to deal with and he respected that and didn't question her. Little did he know just how painful those memories were for her.

On the surface she had seemed happy and content and at peace on the ranch. Looking back now he realized that she had been content to watch the young riders, but had kept her distance from them. Not once had she shown an interest in riding again or even involving herself with the horses other than occasionally scratching or petting a nose that hung over a stall door as she passed.

He had assumed that the memories of the accident and losing Gabri were just too painful. She had walked away from riding and had not shown any interest in doing so again. He respected that and never asked or questioned her reasons. She was back and they were together and that was all that mattered to him. Seeing her happy, laughing, and enjoying herself to the fullest meant the world to him. She wasn't a kid anymore. She was a beautiful, gorgeous, sexy and alluring woman that stirred something so deep inside of him that he never knew existed. No other woman had ever made him feel that way before.

When his phoned vibrated against the glass desktop Mike almost jumped out of his chair in a panic to reach for it. Snatching the phone up he saw the message from Andre that simply read, *"Stopped to get something to eat."*

Mike glared down at the phone furious that Andre had not called instead. He wanted to know how Alexa was doing. "Dammit Andre," he said out loud as he tossed the phone back down onto the desk and kicked his chair backwards.

He wanted to talk to her. He wanted to know how she was doing. He wanted to hear her voice and know that she was alright. He couldn't take the waiting and wondering anymore. He needed to know that she didn't hate him for all the things that he had said. He had let her leave and thought it was the best thing for her own good at the time. But it was Andre that refused to let her run away again.

On his feet, pacing around the corner of the large mahogany desk, he grabbed his phone again. Enough was enough and he hit the call button on Andre's contact icon. Mike listened as the phone rang several times before going to Andre's voicemail and he hung up.

"Fuck Andre, answer your damn phone!" He now knew how Andre must have felt all those years ago but that gave him little solace at this moment so he headed to the built-in bar to fix himself a drink.

He watched the amber colored liquid swirl around the ice cubes like a vortex and knew the burn of the first sip coating his throat would be a welcome pain of distraction. He was on his second glass when his phone rang.

"Why the hell haven't you called?" Mike demanded before Andre even had a chance to speak.

"Look, I only have a minute. Alexa went to the restroom and I don't want her to come back and find me on the phone."

"What is wrong?" Mike felt like the wind had been kicked out of him.

"She is lost in her own world right now — you know that when she shuts down emotionally, the best thing you can do is give her space."

"I thought that she would be happy…"

"She hasn't said much at all, hard to tell just what is going through her mind. I thought she would have been too and for a moment she was…" Andre's voice trailed off and Mike could hear the trepidation in his words. "I have to go. We will be there soon enough."

This wasn't what Mike had been prepared to hear. He had hoped and prayed that Andre could talk her into coming back home where she belonged and together they could sort everything out. He wanted to see her smiling and laughing and happy again. Instead, this was like history repeating itself only their positions were reversed. Maybe he had been right. Maybe they should have let her go for her own reasons and not their selfish desires.

She wasn't a pull toy in a game of tug-of-war. They had both unknowingly hurt her in the past and unwittingly hurt her again. It was evident now, how much they both loved her and she had made her feelings clear to both of them. She loved them both and wouldn't choose one over the other. She had rather walk away instead, leaving them both behind. Either way, they would all three lose.

.

CHAPTER 22

As Alexa headed towards their table she could see Andre putting his phone face down on the table. She knew without a doubt that he had been talking to Mike and from the strained look on his face it wasn't reassuring. She should have gotten on the plane as she had intended. But somewhere deep inside of her she had wanted to stay. She was tired of trying to outrun the past, sick of pretending that her world was this big wonderful fairy tale. She hated being alone and she had missed them both so much over the years. She was tired of hiding who she really was inside.

With Mike she could be free to explore eve-rything she had ever wanted to experience but was too afraid to try. In Andre's arms she felt safe, loved and needed. She needed them both. She wanted it all to go back to the way it was before the accident, before her whole world crumbled in a split second. Mike gave her courage and challenged her to reach outside of her comfort zone. Andre gave her peace, comfort, and the feeling of safety that she so desperately craved. Her childhood had not been an easy one and both Mike and Andre were like older brothers that she never had.

They had made a great team growing up. During her teenage years she had become rebellious and often resented them both at times for treating her like a little sister. Being young and foolish she had made so many mistakes; mistakes that she now had to face. Running away had seemed like the only solution back then.   And twelve hours ago, it seemed like the only solution again.

Now they were headed back to the only place she had ever really considered home but she was dreading the confrontation. She'd give any-thing to turn back time and go back to the way it was before everything had spun out of control. That wasn't possible and she had no answers. Her mind and emotions were a jumbled, tangled mess.

Andre sat quietly next to her as he drove without expecting or demanding anything of her. He had always been the steadying, calming rock that she clung to in the storm. Mike was a different story; he would want answers and try to solve all of the world's problems before he would rest.

Alexa gazed out of the window, watching the mile markers fly by, each one closing the distance between them and the storm she knew she needed to face. She could feel the tension and anxiety building and the muscles in her shoulders and neck were becoming knotted cords of resistance.

She tried rolling her neck from side to side and rolling her shoulders around in circles to help ease the tension. She felt Andre reach over and began to rub and massage the back of her neck and she closed her eyes and let his firm but gentle hands soothe the ache.

"We're almost home. Just relax, everything will work itself out."

Easing into his touch, Alexa never opened her eyes when she felt the truck make the sharp right-hand turn onto the road leading up to the ranch. She knew every twist and turn by heart.

"Can you drive me up to the cabin? I need to rest. I just want to sleep."

"You got it," Andre replied as he turned the truck onto the side road that lead past the barns and up towards the guesthouse, heading away from the main house. When they reached the guesthouse Andre turned off the truck and reached over to take Alexa's hand in his. He brought her hand up to his lips and gently kissed the back of her hand, it seemed so small cradled inside of his own. Alexa reached over with her other hand and touched his cheek. "Thank-you," Alexa stated in a soft quiet tone.

"Wait here and let me make sure that everything is up to par inside. I'll have Maria come up and make sure that the kitchen is stocked."

Maria had been Mike's housekeeper for years and Alexa knew that she kept the guesthouse in immaculate condition and always ready for unexpected guests that frequently dropped by the ranch on business. On her first few trips back to the ranch she had insisted on staying in the guesthouse instead of the main house. Mike hadn't protested and as their relationship grew she spent all of her time at the main house, eventually giving up the safety and solitude of the guesthouse and moving into the Master suite and Mike's bed.

Alexa opened the passenger door and stepped down out of the truck collecting her purse from the floorboard before opening the back door to grab her bags. As she shut both doors, Andre came around the side of the truck and reached for her luggage.

"Let's get you settled," Andre said as he led the way up the cobblestone walkway that led to the front steps.

Entering the spacious rustic log-cabin, Alexa could feel the tension easing in her body. She wanted to curl up in the big four-poster bed and sink into the goose-down mattress top and sleep. Walking into the bedroom the first thing she noticed was that Andre had already turned down the covers on the bed and she could hear the sound of the water running in the whirlpool bathtub.

"You are something else," Alexa smiled up at him.

"So are you," Andre replied as he put her things down next to the walk-in closet, and then walked over to take her into his arms and hold her. Alexa leaned into his chest and returned the embrace.

"We better turn the water off before we flood the place," Alexa said.

"Yeh, I guess we'd better…" Andre leaned down softly kissing her forehead before releasing her and heading for the bathroom suite to turn off the water. He reached in to test the temperature, added a few drops of lavender scented bubble bath and pressed the button to turn on the jets.

Alexa had already unpacked her make-up and toiletries bag from her rolling case and had her robe draped over her shoulder when he returned.

Andre bit his lip at the sight of her standing there. All he really wanted to do at that moment was carry her to the bathroom undress her and sink in the tub behind her. He had loved doing that; washing her back and her hair, drying her off before scooping her up and carrying her to bed.

"Enjoy your bath and try to get some rest. No one will disturb you up here. I'll make sure of it." Andre gave her one last kiss on her cheek as he passed and headed for the doorway.

"Andre we really need to talk. There is so much that I want to say."

Andre stopped in the doorway and turned around. "I'd like that, but not now. You need to rest. We'll have plenty of time later after you have calmed down and gotten a good night's sleep."

"Thank-you again for bringing me home."

"Sweet dreams Honey." Andre turned the lock on the door knob before closing the door behind him.

Alexa listened to his footsteps on the wooden floor until she heard him lock and close the front door before heading to the bathroom to soak away the stress in the whirlpool.

CHAPTER 23

Andre turned the truck around and headed to the main house. He knew Mike was going to be furious because he had brought Alexa to the cabin but that was too damn bad. He was going to have to get over it.

He would call Maria later after Alexa had time to settle in and hopefully fall asleep. Maria wouldn't disturb her and he wanted to make sure that Alexa had everything she needed so that she didn't have to leave the cabin until she was ready. He knew all of her favorite snacks and comfort foods by heart and he made a mental list to give to Maria.

He had just turned onto the driveway leading up to the main house when his phone went off. "Where the hell are you? And where is Alexa? I saw your truck heading up the road over forty-five minutes ago."

Andre knew what Mike was thinking and he ought to let him stew in it. "I am pulling up to the house now," Andre answered him and ended the call.

Entering the house through the back door, Andre took his time wiping his boots on the rough coconut husk doormat. Instead of heading straight for Mike's office, Andre went to the kitchen.

Pulling a large glass out of the cabinet he went to the refrigerator, held the glass against the button on the door and listened to the ice clink against the glass. Opening the opposite door he reached in for the pitcher of iced tea and filled the glass. Leaning against the island counter, still holding the pitcher, Andre took two large swallows and felt the ice cold liquid begin to quench his thirst. It had been one hell of a morning and in his rush between getting to the ranch, then heading to the airport and back, he hadn't taken the time to think about stopping long enough to even grab a bottle of water. Andre refilled the glass before returning the pitcher to the refrigerator and closing the door.

He didn't know what the solution was — but he damned sure knew what it wasn't. He and Mike had been working in tandem to build this ranch for over thirty years and they had disagreed many of times on various issues but they had always managed to work out their differences and come to an agreement that was in the best interest of the business, not letting their pride or need to be right, destroy what they had worked so hard to build. In all the years, they had never let their disagreements erode their friendship. Like brothers, they had had their share of ugly spats over the years but Mike was the only 'family' that Andre had and whatever their differences were, it was not worth losing that brotherhood bond.

But when it came to Alexa — this was an entirely different matter. It would be the ultimate test of their friendship. Andre would not back down this time. She was not going to be pulled between the two of them like a ragdoll. He would make sure of that. Refilling his glass one last time, Andre headed for Mike's office.

Andre didn't bother knocking on the closed door before opening it and walking in. Mike was behind his desk on his phone when Andre set his glass on the desk, pulled up a chair and waited.

"I agree totally. I will have my corporate secretary fax all the necessary paperwork over to your office and we can go from there," Mike answered. "Cal, I have someone who just walked into my office and I need to go over some things with them. I can give you a call later tonight or tomorrow after you have had a chance to go over the paperwork. We can discuss the options in more detail then." Mike stated. "Yes, yes it was great talking to you — I look forward to working with you on this project as well. We'll keep in touch." Mike ended the call and set his phone on the desk.

Staring at Andre, Mike leaned back in his chair and ran both of his hands through his hair, taking a deep breath before returning his chair to an upright position and facing Andre head on. "Why did you bring Alexa up to the cabin?" Mike started.

"Because that is where she wanted to go," Andre answered.

"I wanted you to bring her here!"

"It isn't about what you wanted and you need to get that through your head!" Andre challenged, slamming his glass down on the desk.

"Andre, take it easy. I was worried and when I saw your truck heading towards the cabin it made me furious."

"I know damn well what you were thinking. You of all people should know me better than that. Alexa is not a possession. She wanted to go to the cabin and that is where I brought her."

Mike settled into his chair, his elbows resting on the desk leaning forward to face Andre. "How is she?"

"She is exhausted. Emotionally drained and worn out. I tried to get her to eat at the restaurant but she just picked at her meal, moving things around with her fork but not eating."

Mike leaned back and stared up at the ceiling.

"Look Mike, she needs to rest. She needs time to process everything. Reopening all of the old wounds and scars of the past has left her a wreck. Granted, neither one of us knew how deep those wounds were, but ripping away all of her defenses has left her raw and hurting. She spent twenty-five years running away from those memories — from this ranch — from both of us."

"Andre, you don't understand. For the last two years she was the happiest that I had ever seen her."

"No, you don't understand. That person was the Alexa that had risen above her past, reinvented herself, and risen above the wounds that she had long ago locked inside of herself. When you reopened that box, everything came flying back at her so fast that she couldn't build the cement walls fast enough and was left with the searing pain of those repressed memories. Now she has to deal with them."

"Did she say anything on the ride back?"

"Nope. Not a word."

"She didn't try to explain or even mention the baby?"

"No. And unlike you, I am ok with that. If and when she is ready to talk about it, she will."

"Andre have you noticed the locket she wears?" Mike asked.

"Yes, why? Where are you going with this Mike?" Andre asked, confused by Mike's switch in tone and questions.

"Did you look at the locket?"

"No. I noticed it but it never crossed my mind with everything else going on. What are you getting at?"

"Andre, it was more than just a miscarriage that she suffered through. I didn't know that at the time, but after she told me about the baby — I called a friend of mine who is an OB/GYN — I needed to know and understand what had happened."

Andre leaned forward in his chair not knowing if he wanted to hear anymore but too shocked to not know. "And…"

"The night I acted like such an ass, Alexa let me see the locket. The front has an angel engraved on it." Mike paused to let his words sink in for a moment. "Inside the locket there are two tiny foot prints stamped on a card." Mike watched the blood drain from his best friend's face as the realization hit home. "On the back, the name 'Tyler' is engraved along with the date of the accident." Mike finished.

"She named him…it was a boy?" Andre slumped back in his chair.

"Yes. They even let her see him."

"I am not understanding this…She didn't even look pregnant. This isn't making any sense."

"Andre, how long before the accident had it been since you two were alone together?"

"Are you asking me how long it had been since we had slept together?" Andre snapped back.

"Not exactly. How long had it been since you had seen her in anything but an oversized sweatshirt and yoga pants?"

"Two months before the accident — she just up and decided to call off the relationship — without so much as an explanation."

"That makes more sense now."

"Maybe to you. But I don't understand a damn thing you are talking about. Or why we are even having this conversation."

"In the hospital she had been so adamant about not wanting anyone around her and not even wanting me to call her parents. Looking back, it all adds up now."

"The hell it does."

"Andre just listen to me for a minute and hear me out." Mike waited for a minute and then continued. "The reason I called my friend was because I needed answers. I didn't understand it all either. None of it was adding up. Not what Alexa was saying. Not what went on in the hospital. Not what the doctors and nurses had said. None of it. I needed to understand — so I called him."

"And?"

"And I told him what I did know. Everything, including the locket and the foot prints."

"What the hell did he say?"

"Given the nature of her fall and the fact that she had a broken pelvis meant that it had most likely caused permanent trauma to the baby. Since Alexa had been allowed to see the baby and had the stamped card with his foot prints, meant that she would have had to deliver the baby."

"What?" Andre stared at Mike in disbelief.

"Are you understanding what I am telling you?" Mike leaned forward to rest his forearms on the desk. "I was wrong for not calling you. I admit that now. But I had no idea just how much she was dealing with or why she kept me away."

Andre stood up almost knocking the chair backwards as he turned his back on Mike and crossed the room towards the wet bar that was built into the corner of the office. Bracing himself with his outstretched arms, he gripped the edge of the bar until his knuckles turned white.

Mike crossed the room to the bar, pulled out two rock glasses, filled them with ice and poured them each a drink and handed one to Andre.

"Why are you telling me this, why?" Andre took the glass from Mike's hand.

"So that she doesn't have to — I don't want her to have to relive the nightmare yet again."

"You mean to tell me that she actually had to go into labor and deliver the baby...Our baby...alone?" Andre grabbed the bottle and poured another drink slamming that one down and refilling the glass again.

"I am afraid so, and it rips my heart out to know that I was right there and she wouldn't say anything or even let me near her. If I would have known about your relationship I would have called you. I was only focused on her physical injuries and had no clue what she was going through emotionally."

"Son of a bitch. I can't believe that she made those decisions alone without even letting you comfort or console her. We both know how stubborn she is but that is ridiculous! And for her to not even tell me about the baby in the first place!"

"Andre getting angry with her now will only make things worse. That is why I am telling you all of this so that you can rationally process it, vent your anger and not upset her any further."

"But why would she not tell me she was pregnant in the first place. I would have done everything and anything for her. She had to know that."

"Maybe after what Brent pulled, she couldn't bear to have you turn your back on her too."

"Don't ever compare me to Brent. I loved her and would have married her and been so happy to know that she was carrying our child."

"She didn't know that."

"I have to tell her. I need her to know."

"Not now. Not until you have processed your own feelings and dealt with your own anger. And not until she is ready."

"So now what"

"She is here. She is safe. And I don't want her to run away again so we go back to the way things used to be before we fucked everything up. We give her space, watch over her like we used to and hopefully she opens up and trusts us again."

"You know she will resent the hell out of us if we start treating her like a kid again."

"I didn't mean it like that." Mike poured himself another drink and went back to sit in his chair letting the alcohol soothe his nerves. "The office in the guesthouse is fully wired. I'll have it set-up so that she can work from there if she chooses. And I would like to see her ride again."

"Are you nuts? She avoids the barns like the plague."

"I realize that but now that I know the reason, I think getting her riding again would be good for her — one step towards recovery. It isn't the horses that she is afraid of, it is the memories."

"I am not sure about that."

"I am. I've watched her walk through the barn and not be able to resist stopping to scratch a nose or gently pet the ones hanging over their stall doors. I've seen how she watches the young riders in the practice arena."

"That is a long way from actually getting her to ride again."

"How far along is the Friesian mare?" Mike asked.

"The dapple grey Holsteiner would be a better choice."

"I thought about that but I think it would remind her too much of Gabri. She always loved the Friesians but back then she wasn't experienced enough. Now I think the challenge is just what she needs."

"The Friesian mare has a long way to go. She is a good mount but a handful."

"Get one of the trainers to start working her and getting her into condition."

"No. If you have in mind to get Alexa to ride her — than I will do it myself. I won't put her on a horse that I don't feel she is ready for this soon. My God Mike, she hasn't ridden since the accident."

"No one said Alexa would agree to ride again but at least if she would start with some of the groundwork it may build her confidence back-up."

"The Friesian is a gorgeous mare. The grooms dread fooling with her because of the amount time and work it takes."

"That's my point. Alexa has always loved and admired the breed and I think it would spark her interest and get her back in the barns again. Even if she just handled the grooming, it would be a start."

"You have a point." Andre agreed. Andre knew Mike had switched the subject on purpose to give him time to cool off and get his emotions under control. But he also knew Mike well enough to know that he had been carefully considering this for a while, probably even before everything had blown up. Mike rarely involved himself in the training operations and Andre could tell that he had been doing his research on this one. It had not been a spur of the moment decision.

Andre would love to see Alexa riding again but he had his doubts about the timing. Then again, maybe it was just the challenge she needed right now to get her mind off of everything else for a while. Andre was grateful that Mike had switched subjects to allow him to regain his balance but there was still more he needed to know and wouldn't be able to let it go until he had the answers. Every instinct in his body made him want to rush up to the cabin to hold her and tell her how sorry he had been and to try to make it all up to her.

"Does she have everything she needs up at the guesthouse?" Mike asked.

"I had planned on calling Maria and it slipped my mind with everything."

"I'll call her."

"No let me call her. Alexa may have gotten used to your style of gourmet cuisine but I know the comfort foods that she craves when she is in a funk." Andre fished his phone out of his pocket to call Maria but he saw Mike grin and they both had to laugh at the fact that at least some things had never changed.

"Well if she is up and hungry, the one thing she won't refuse is a medium-well rib-eye steak."

"You are right on that one."

"She will eat it cold out of the refrigerator." Mike grinned.

"That she will. I have no idea how she does that but you are right."

"I have two defrosted in the fridge. Why don't I cook them while you call Maria — then you can bring them up to the cabin and check on her. I'm worried about her and want to make sure she gets something in her stomach. She won't turn down a rib-eye."

"Or chocolate and pretzels." Andre added.

Mike just shook his head and grinned as he headed to the kitchen to start the indoor grill, leaving Andre alone to call Maria. Closing the door behind him Mike had to admit to himself how very different Alexa was with each of them. It had always been that way from the beginning.

Andre had a way of soothing and comforting her and if they both had any chance of getting her to stay on at the ranch, Mike was going to have to shelf his pride and do whatever it took to make her feel at home again. Either they worked this out or they would lose her forever. As much as it hurt, he needed to give them both time to mend the wounds of the past before they could decide what to do about the future. He had expected Andre to bring Alexa straight to the house. He hadn't even considered the idea of her staying up at the cabin. He had also been hoping that Alexa would talk to Andre about the baby but that didn't happen either.

Mike had made the decision to tell Andre himself because he needed him to know. If Alexa was still not ready to talk about it he could understand that, but Andre needed to know. By telling Andre himself, Mike hoped it would ease some of the tension between them and spare Alexa the pain of telling Andre herself. She had only told him because he had prodded and pushed her past her breaking point, he didn't want that to happen again. He had seen the pain in Andre's face and the raw emotions that came with it. It had been the right choice. It was better to let Andre have time to process his own emotions and pain instead of allowing him to blow up on Alexa the way he himself had done.

If Mike had only known the whole truth he never would have said the things that he had said. He didn't want Andre to make the same mistake and cause Alexa any more pain than she was already dealing with.

"Something smells damn good," Andre said.

Mike had just finished packing the containers when Andre walked into the kitchen.

"You had better take it up there while it is still hot," Mike replied, handing the insulated bag to Andre.

"Aren't you eating?" Andre questioned.

"I will grab a bite later," Mike replied as he stacked the dishes into the sink. "Make sure she eats Andre. Even, if you have to feed it to her bite by bite. There is a chilled bottle of wine in there as well. She will enjoy that and it will help take the edge off of her nerves."

"I will. And Mike...Thank-you!"

"You had better get moving before I change my mind and bring it up there myself."

CHAPTER 24

Alexa heard the crunching sound of the gravel as the pick-up pulled into the driveway. She had been stretched out on the large plush sofa reading, grateful for the quiet solitude of the cabin. She had been sleeping when she had heard Maria moving around the kitchen earlier, but she had waited until Maria left before getting up and pulling on a pair of sweatpants and a t-shirt.

She had wandered into the kitchen in search of something to snack on; when she had inspected the contents of the refrigerator and cabinets, there hadn't been a doubt who was responsible for the selection. She had fished out a can of soda from the fridge, a bag of pretzels from the pantry and grabbed a tin of her favorite dark mint chocolate pearls and headed back to the living room.

Hearing the pinging sound of the open truck door, she was glad that she had gotten dressed earlier. She had been anticipating and dreading having Mike barge into the cabin and demand to know why she had not gone to the house. Glancing out of the large picture window, she noticed that it was Andre's truck parked out front and not Mike's and she breathed a sigh of relief. She could hear his footsteps crossing the wide porch and the tone of each number as he punched in the code on the keypad to unlock the door.

"Hey, you're up? I was afraid to disturb you." Andre said, balancing the bags he was carrying, trying not to spill the contents before he reached the kitchen.

"What do you have in there? Maria already stocked the kitchen while I was asleep." Alexa questioned as she rose from the sofa and crossed the room to help him with the bags he was toting. "Something smells good."

"I hope so. Not sure what all is in here. Mike had it packed before I was ready to leave."

"Smells like steak to me." Alexa grinned as she helped him unpack the containers from the bags.

"We bet on the fact that you wouldn't turn down a good steak."

"You know it." Alexa skipped the formalities, dug a fork and knife out of the drawer and started popping the lids off of the divided containers to inspect the contents. "And steak it is…" Alexa smiled up at him before going in search of the Worcestershire sauce, while Andre slid two wine glasses from the overhead rack and uncorked the bottle of Moscato wine that Mike had chosen.

Red wine goes with steak but it was a debate that both he and Mike had long given up on. Alexa liked what she liked and didn't much care what the experts thought, so he grinned to himself when he saw Mike's choice.

Alexa was already perched cross-legged on top of one of the tall four-legged stools, drowning her steak in Worcestershire sauce, when he sat her wine glass in front of her and pulled up at stool on the opposite side of the butcher-block island. Cutting into his own steak, he watched her as she ate and noticed the locket dangling from the thin silver chain around her neck. He was glad to see her eating and smiling but all he could focus on was the locket.

He wanted to hold it. He wanted to touch it and open it. He wanted to hold her in his arms and tell her how sorry he was for not being there with her.

"The steak is awesome. Thank-you so much." Alexa stated.

"You will have to thank Mike. They were his doing."

"Is he upset because I came up here?"

"He was, at first." Andre chose his words carefully.

"I was expecting him to come flying up here mad as hell."

"Oh he wanted to." Andre answered her.

"I'm sure he did. What changed his mind?"

"I told him that it was your choice and he needed to respect that." Andre wasn't comfortable with the direction the conversation was heading and he didn't trust his own emotions as he could feel them rising up from the pit of his stomach. "Mike tells me that you have been admiring the Friesian mare we have in the barn."

"She is a gorgeous animal. I have been down to watch her work several times."

"What do you think about her?"

"I think she is rough around the edges and still flighty but she has great potential with the right trainer and rider."

"She is a handful and a power house. Most of the staff aren't crazy about working with her."

"Why?"

"She is absolutely stunning to look at but she can be stubborn and hardheaded, kind of like someone else I know."

"Well if they knew what they were doing, they would see past that and realize her potential. She isn't clicking with the trainers and handlers you have her with. They fight against each other and don't work as a team."

Andre could tell by her comments that Mike had been right. Her irritated tone made it obvious that she thought the mare wasn't being given a chance to prove herself. And it meant that she had been carefully studying the mare for some time.

"Maybe you're right. I hadn't thought about it. I haven't had the chance to really watch her work or handle her myself since I got back." Andre was studying her reaction to see if she would give him an opening to suggest that she might be willing to work with the mare.

"You need to work with her before taking their opinions and dismissing her. She reminds me so much of Gentlemen's Coach that Mike was riding when I when I first saw him compete."

"I remember him well. In fact the mare is out of the same bloodline." Andre waited, watching her facial expressions as the wheels in her head started turning.

"Then why isn't she being worked by one of the more experienced trainers?"

"Because they have their hands full with the high-dollar horses that the owners are paying us to train and most of them prefer the lighter, quicker breeds."

"So she belongs to the ranch?" Alexa questioned. Andre watched her perk up at the fact that the mare was owned by the ranch and not an outsider.

"Yes. She is out of one of Mike's private bloodlines. She just turned four years old."

"I have seen her work. She has great potential."

"We'll see what she has in her once I get a chance to work with her myself." Andre stated and decided to leave the conversation there and let Alexa mull over it. He had peaked her interest and had watched her reactions. All they had to do was wait until she came to her own decision.

Andre refilled their glasses and gazed back at the locket. She had finished her steak and was pushing the vegetables around her plate. Everything in his brain told him not to go there, but everything in his heart begged to be let out. As she put her fork down and moved her plate to the side. Andre reached across the table for her hand. He felt her tense up when he first gripped her hand in his, and then she eased up letting her hand relax into his as she reached for her glass with her opposite hand.

"Alexa, would you look at me for a minute? Mike told me about the baby and about the locket." He immediately felt her tense up and try to pull her hand away from his. "Alexa, please don't pull away. Don't shut me out." Andre pleaded.

"Mike had no right to do that." Alexa stammered but she didn't withdraw her hand.

"You named him Tyler. That was my grandfather's name."

"I know." Alexa answered him.

"Let's leave the dishes and go for a walk. It is a beautiful night — the sky is clear — the stars are out and the fresh air will do us both some good." Andre released her hand as he stood up from his seat and circled around the island to gather her into his arms. Hugging her tightly to his chest, he smoothed her long wavy hair that fell gently down her back. Alexa uncrossed her legs and moved off of her stool to return his embrace.

Through his shirt, Andre could feel the locket pressing into his skin. Reaching his hand under her hair to caress her neck, he let the thin chain slide through his fingers. Unable to resist his own emotions, he continued to follow the chain down its length until the locket rested between his fingers. Rubbing it between his thumb and forefinger Andre could feel the engravings.

"Will you show it to me?" Andre asked as he continued to rub his finger in a circle over the letters that marked the name of the baby they had created and the date he had been taken from them.

"He was so tiny Andre — and when they took him from me…"

Andre could feel her tears on his chest and the ones welling up in his own eyes.

"They wrapped him in a blanket and let me hold him. He fit in my hand — but he was perfect." Alexa curled into Andre's chest and he closed his arms around her even tighter, fighting his own emotions. Cradling her in his embrace he gently rocked her as he listened to her. He had wanted to know but hearing her tell him was breaking his heart. Knowing that she had had to face it all alone was killing him inside.

"I am so sorry I was not there for you."

"Oh Andre…" Alexa murmured between sobs.

"Why Honey? Why didn't you tell me?"

"I couldn't. I just couldn't. I was so afraid — I didn't know what to do." Alexa's whole body was trembling as the sobs turned into wracking cries.

"Shhh Honey, I've got you...let it all go. You don't have to keep hiding it anymore. It's ok." Andre rocked her gently and softly kissed her forehead. "I'm here. I am right here and I'm not going anywhere."

"I thought you would leave me if you found out. I didn't know what to do and I panicked. It was easier for me to break it off — than to face your rejection if you knew."

"Oh, Alexa..." Andre didn't even try to stop the tears that crept out the corners of his eyes. "I never would have left you. Never. I would have been so happy and so proud to know of the life we had created."

"But I failed — I failed in that too — and lost him..." Alexa stammered, her words coming out in bursts between the sobs.

"No you didn't fail. The accident was not your fault. Don't think like that, please don't believe that."

"I was so ashamed."

"Please Honey don't ever feel that way. If I had known..." Alexa's body had become so weak in his arms from crying and in one swift motion Andre reached down and scooped her legs up into his arms, carrying her into the living room. With her curled in his arms, Andre settled them both into the sofa and held her in his lap. Laying her head on the armrest of the sofa, Andre gently brushed her hair out of her eyes and wiped her tear-stained cheeks, placing his other hand over the locket that rested on her chest.

"That is all that I have left to remind me that he existed. That he was real."

"Can I see it?" Andre moved his hand to uncover the locket and gazed down at the silver oval pendant and could clearly see the engraved face of the tiny angel on the lid.

Alexa lifted the locket, placed it in his hand, and unlatched the clip opening the locket, exposing the two tiny foot prints.

Andre immediately felt the hot sting of tears as they flooded his eyes. Staring down at the prints of his son's feet, he let the tears that he had been fighting to hold back, run down his face as he hung on to Alexa pulling her tighter and tighter into his chest.

Holding onto each other, Andre and Alexa both let go of the emotional pain that had tormented them for the past twenty-five years.

It was well after midnight when Andre opened his eyes, feeling Alexa move in his lap. They had fallen asleep in each other's arms. Without wanting to wake her, Andre hooked an arm under her bent knees and the other around her shoulders, lifting her into his arms to carry her to bed where she could stretch out and sleep in the comfort of the goose-down mattress. As he settled her into the huge bed, Alexa stirred and clung to his shirt.

"Don't leave me. Please Andre, don't leave…"

"Shhh…I'm right here. Go back to sleep and rest."

"Don't leave. Please don't leave me alone."

Intending only to comfort her back to sleep, Andre lifted her up, gently moving her into the middle of the bed giving him room to curl up next to her. Alexa curled into his arms with her back pressed against his chest as Andre covered her with the sheet and tucked it around her. Andre curled his tall frame around her body, gently massaging her shoulder until they both fell asleep.

CHAPTER 25

Mike was up before sunrise having been unable to sleep and was out on the balcony with his first cup of coffee cursing the daybreak and first light as it rose over the hills surrounding the barns. From his vantage point he could see Andre's truck still parked outside the guesthouse and it felt like a hot knife twisting inside him.

His brain was telling him that he had made the right decision last night, but this morning his heart didn't believe a word of it. Seeing Andre's truck parked outside the guesthouse was something he had dreaded the most and the thoughts that had kept him awake all night. Mike knew that Andre

and Alexa had needed the time alone to sort everything out but he had not been prepared for what that
would ultimately lead to. He had honestly believed
that Andre would do the right thing and not take
advantage of the vulnerable state Alexa was in, now
he knew how wrong he had been and he was mad as
hell.

Mike had misjudged the situation and now
regretted it as he continued to focus on the sight of
the truck. Andre damned well knew better.   They
had both agreed to give her the time she needed to
heal the scars that still plagued her. He had wanted
them to talk. He had wanted them to be able sort out
the past. But he damn well had not wanted to see
that pick-up still sitting in the driveway when the
sun came up.

His first instinct had been to grab his
phone; his second instinct had been to grab his keys
and head up there, but he had done neither. Instead,
he stood there and watched the sun rise higher in
the sky with no signs of Andre emerging from the
cabin with even a pretense of sneaking out before
daybreak. The grooms and handlers were all starting to arrive, some already moving horses in and

around the paddock areas. The sight of Andre's truck wouldn't go unnoticed.

As angry as he was, he would not give Andre the satisfaction of acting like nothing had happened. He had not known about their relationship back then, but he did now and that fact he could no longer deny. Alexa had made it clear how she felt, and now he knew that Andre had no intention of letting her go again. That, Mike would deal with later. Right now, he had no intention of letting the gossip run through the barns like wildfire behind his back.

Andre might be in charge of the training operation, but he owned the ranch and he would let that fact be known.

When Mike walked into the main barn, grooms and stable-hands scattered in the opposite direction. They were not used to seeing Mike in the barns anymore unless he was on a mission. Having Mike present in the barn usually meant trouble. Many of the newer employees had never seen Mike ride, but they knew who signed their paychecks.

Mike headed straight towards the trainer's lounge area, adjacent to Andre's office, merely nodding at those he passed. As Mike entered the lounge, several of the trainers stood up from the tables where they had been eating their breakfast and discussing the training schedules for the day. Mike acknowledged them with a terse 'Good Morning', before turning his attention towards Owen who was still seated behind his desk in the far corner of the room.

Owen was Andre's head trainer and was quite capable of handling the operation in Andre's absence. Owen had been on the ranch for almost ten years and was a topnotch trainer and experienced rider at all levels with several Grand Prix championships to his credit. He hadn't been Mike's first choice for the position, but Andre had believed in his experience and trusted him.

"Good Morning Mike," Owen greeted him as he reached out to shake Mike's hand. "We don't get to see you much on this side. What's up?"

"Who is assigned to the four year old Friesian mare?" Mike questioned him.

"No one in particular. The trainers pretty much rotate, depending on who has the free time to work with her." Owen answered.

"I want you to assign your best groom, handler, and trainer to her regimen, and I want her looking in top condition."

"You have a buyer coming in?"

"No, a rider," Mike answered.

"Better be a dam good one, that's for sure."

"She was one of the best." Mike stated.

"She? Have you lost your mind? That mare is a beast to work with, even my most experienced trainers don't like working with her."

"Andre will oversee her training, but for now, starting today, I want her exercised daily and looking like a million bucks. I also want her moved to a stall in the main stable with her own paddock."

"Mike, there isn't a free stall with a paddock in the front stable."

"Find one." Mike answered.

"Andre will throw a fit if I start moving horses around without consulting him. Especially, in the front stable."

Turning his attention to one of the other lead trainers, Mike gave his order. "Go get the mare and bring her up here. I want to see how she moves around the schooling pen on a lunge line." Without hesitation, the trainer left the lounge.

"Mike, with all due respect, Andre reserves the front stable for only the top level horses. Housing a young horse up there isn't going to sit well with him at all. Not to mention the fact that you are planning to put a young inexperienced rider on that mare. I just don't agree with the logic or reasoning behind this."

"I don't pay you to second guess my logic or reasoning or decisions. You have made an error in your assumption that I was bringing in an inexperienced rider. That is not what I told you. And you are also mistaken in your assumption that Andre will challenge my judgment." Mike towered over Owen's desk making his orders clear. After giving the trainer a minute to let his words sink in and realize that his orders weren't up for debate, Mike backed off. "Come with me for a minute," Mike said and he turned around to head out of the lounge as Owen stood up to follow him.

Punching in the code on the keypad, Mike unlocked Andre's office door and flipped on the light switch. Giving Owen a chance to catch up,

Mike crossed the room to the far wall where Andre had hung countless framed photographs taken over the years when they had both been competing. Mike hadn't actually looked at them in years, but now standing there, he could recall each photo and the memory it captured like it was yesterday.

There were so many of the three of them together. The expressions on their faces showed how happy and proud they had been. Mike reached up to run his hand over one in particular; it was the last one taken of the three of them before the accident. Turning back to address Owen who was just standing in the middle of the office, "Do you have any clue who this is?" Mike questioned him.

Owen walked over to look at the framed image that Mike was referring to; never making the connection between the petite brunette that he had occasionally seen around the barn and the framed pictures hanging on the walls of Andre's office. "That is Alexa Connor, I've heard Andre speak of her many times over the years. I never had the privilege of meeting her in person or seeing her ride, but her reputation as one of the elites was well known when I first started riding. I knew she was one of your teammates."

"She was more than just a teammate — she lived and breathed for this ranch and this sport." Staring at the photographs tempered Mike's anger as he remembered what it was like back then before their world had been turned inside out. Mike stroked the frame of the picture one last time before abruptly turning away from the wall of memories and headed for the door, realizing that Owen still had not made the connection.

"I want to show you something else you don't know," Mike said as he turned out the lights, closed the door and headed down the opposite alleyway towards the tack rooms. When Mike reached the door to what had been Alexa's private tack room he reached into his pocket for the key, noticing the puzzled look on Owen's face. Only three people had a key to this lock. This time he turned on the lights but let Owen enter the room first.

Along one wall was a huge built-in glass trophy case surround with more framed photos. In the center of the wall, above the trophy case was a

16 X 20 photograph of Alexa and Gabri. There was a brass plaque attached along the bottom edge of the frame engraved with both of their names and the date it was taken. It was the day that she had won her first Grand Prix freestyle championship.

The end wall supported the saddle racks and hooks that held all of her bridles, bits, halters, and other tack, all neatly arranged and still exactly as she had left it. Four of her riding helmets sat equally spaced along the top of the glass trophy case. Her desk sat on the opposite side of the room, behind it was the door to her private changing room complete with a shower and closet for her boots and outfits. Mike had designed the room himself just for her. He had wanted her to have her privacy and her own space separate from the rest of the tack rooms. Mike ran his hand along the smooth leather seat of one of her favorite saddles. He had kept the room exactly as it was and had made sure all of the gear and room was routinely cleaned, dusted and polished over the years. He had preserved it in immaculate shape with the hopes that she would return one day. There were times when he would come down here late at night to just sit in the room and feel her presence. Only two people knew the room existed and he knew that Andrew often did the same.

"I have never seen this door opened and we have all wondered what was in here," Owen stated in amazement. "All I can say is Wow. This was actually her dressing room and office?"

"Yes, and no one other than Andre or myself is allowed in here." Mike declared.

"Whatever happened to her? The room looks like a shrine. I have been here ten years and never knew it existed yet it looks like it had never been closed."

"I made sure of it." Mike answered. "I wanted it kept exactly the way that she left it."

"She must have been pretty damn important to you." Owen replied.

"She was and still is." Mike answered him before turning around and heading for the door. "Now, back to business..." Mike opened the door, waited for Owen to leave the room, turned out the lights and locked the door behind them. "I was dead serious when I said that I want that mare moved to the front stable, groomed, polished, and in top condition."

"Yes sir. But I am warning you Mike, that mare is a powerhouse and a handful to work." Owen replied.

"That's because she is young and has never been given the attention and proper training that she deserved." Mike snapped back.

"Whatever you say, I just don't think she has the right disposition, especially for a new rider." Owen answered.

"Let me be the judge of that," Mike stated. "I want to see how she moves in the round pen." Mike turned back down the alleyway and headed for the training area.

Alexa and Andre were just walking into the barn when Mike and Owen crossed their path. It took everything that Mike had to keep his anger in check. His reason for deciding to go to the training center this morning was precisely to squelch any rumors before they started. He would deal with Andre later. Right now, this was neither the time nor the place.

"Glad you two showed up," Mike stated.

"I wanted to bring Alexa down to see the mare." Andre replied.

"Well you are in luck; I had the handlers bring her up to the training area earlier this morning. We were just fixing to head over there to watch her in the schooling pen."

"I wasn't at all impressed with the way she was being handled the last time I watched them work her," Alexa interjected. "She reminds me so much of her grandsire and if she is anything like him, she will make an impressive mount given the right handling and training."

Owen started to bow-up at Alexa's criticism of his staff but one look from Mike had silenced any comment that he had been ready to spout off.

"Owen, this is Alexa. She will be around the stables and I want you to inform your staff that she is to come and go as she pleases."

With a stunned look on his face, Owen extended his hand out in greeting, "Alexa Connor? The Alexa Connor?" Owen blurted out. "Mike was just showing me…" and Owen cut his words, not finishing the sentence when Mike glared at him and shook his head, signaling Owen not to say anything further.

"Nice to meet you, Owen." Alexa returned the greeting and reached forward to shake his hand. "Just call me Alexa."

"Very nice to meet you," Owen replied. "Mike I will check to see that the mare is ready." Making a break in the conversation, Owen headed off towards the trainer's lounge.

Mike knew Owen couldn't wait to inform the others of Alexa's presence but that had been his reasoning behind showing him the pictures of her and her tack room; giving them something else to gossip about would keep them busy and distracted from his real reason.

After watching the mare work through the exercises in the schooling pen, Mike agreed with Alexa's assessment. They had not been working the mare properly and he was ticked. Mike had ordered them to bring her to the grooming area where he could inspect her physical condition.

The mare was already on the cross-ties when Mike, Alexa, and Andre entered the grooming area. While Mike ran his hands expertly over the mare's body Alexa reached up to scratch the mare's nose and run her fingers through the long hairs of her forelock. Alexa had always been a fanatic when it came to grooming, even out of season; she had insisted that their horses be kept in show condition. It had been one of her biggest pet peeves. The mare hadn't been clipped in some time and her hair was dry and brittle.

Andre stood back watching Alexa rub the mare's head and noticed how the mare's disposition changed. The two seemed drawn together. He had to admit to himself that Mike had been right. Alexa and the mare seemed to soothe each other.

Finishing his inspection, Mike gave orders to the grooms before stepping back almost stumbling over Alexa. Andre just grinned as the mare tossed her head and stamped one foot down on the cement floor. The mare had become irritated and restless at Mike's sudden movements that ended the gentle stroking she had been enjoying.

"Let's go to the office and discuss a new regimen schedule," Mike said addressing Andre as he steadied Alexa with one hand.

Side by side the three of them walked towards Andre's office. The staff standing around the mare watched the threesome with disbelief. When Owen had told them Alexa Connor was in the stable they hadn't believed him. Many of the younger staff members had no knowledge of who she was but Owen had filled them all in on the history as he knew it, even telling them about her private tack room. For years the locked door had been a complete mystery to all of them and the topic of many jokes about what lay behind that door.

Standing in Andre's office, Alexa turned away from them both and went over to the wall to look at the pictures that represented all the years that they had spent together; looking up at all of their accomplishments brought back so many memories. One by one she stared at each, letting the images retell the events that had brought them all so much happiness.

Behind her Mike and Andre had gotten quiet, watching her reactions as she focused on the images. When Alexa finally turned around Mike and Andre both exhaled in tandem as they saw the smile on her face.

"We had made a great team back then," Alexa said.

"That we had," Andre replied.

"What are your plans for the Friesian?" Alexa asked. "You aren't planning to sell her?"

"Not quite sure yet. I had planned to keep her but none of the trainers or riders have taken any interest in her. Andre and I both have our hands full with the business operations." Mike answered.

"That's because they are damn fools," Alexa replied. "She has all the potential to make it to the top level and beyond. They would be lucky to have the privilege of starting her at this age."

"Her nickname in the stable is The Black Beast," Andre said. "She seems to dislike them as much as they dislike her."

"She doesn't trust them and she senses their attitude with the way they handle her." Alexa responded.

"I can either sell her or keep her as a brood mare," Mike said.

"That is just plain stupid," Alexa stated.

"Well it seems unfair to keep her stalled if she isn't getting worked." Mike dropped the bait hoping Alexa would jump at it.

Andre sat behind his desk, his elbows on the armrest of his chair with his fingers pressed together in a diamond shape, watching the two of them. Mike had always been able to bait her into a new challenge.

"Andre, how long would it take you to have her in sale condition?" Mike asked.

"A couple of weeks max," Andre answered.

"Mike you can't sell her," Alexa insisted.

"It just isn't practical to take up stall space when she isn't being worked." Mike set the hook.

"What if I worked with her for a few months before you make your decision? It is unfair to base your judgment on the trainer's opinion when they haven't even bothered to gain her trust or work her properly." Alexa took the bait.

"I don't know Alexa. You haven't ridden in years and you heard their opinions of her disposition. If you ever want to just ride for pleasure we have a Holsteiner mare that would be perfect," Mike stated.

Andre leaned back in his chair to watch the fireworks. He could tell by Alexa's stance and posture that she had found Mike's offer demeaning, which had been Mike's motive all along.

"I have seen the Holsteiner mare work and she is well-suited for the young inexperienced riders but she will never make it past a mid-level test."

"That is why we keep her around, but she is a joy to ride."

"Give me two months with the Friesian mare and if you aren't satisfied with her progress then you can make your decision."

"You seriously feel up to working with her?" Mike asked.

"She deserves a chance to prove herself." Alexa answered.

"Well if you are up for the challenge I'll give you two months to see what you can do with her. I would love to see you ride again."

"In two months you are going to be glad that you didn't sell her."

"Welcome back Alexa," Mike said.

Having won the debate, Alexa looked at Andre and then back at Mike and knew she had been played. They had been setting her up the whole time. She should have known when Andre had started talking about the mare the night before. Exhausted and emotionally drained, she had just welcomed the change in conversation. When Andre had insisted on coming up to the stable this morning she had assumed that he was just using the excuse as a diversion to get her out of the cabin and get her mind off of everything. She had thought it odd to see Mike's truck at the stable when they pulled up.

"I guess that means a shopping trip into town. I didn't exactly pack for this adventure."

"Not exactly. We have anything you need already at your disposal." Mike answered.

"You know how I feel about borrowing or using anyone else's tack."

"I'm sure we can come up with something that will suit the purpose for now. Let's go see what is available and then you can make a shopping list of what you might need." Mike motioned for Andre to follow them.

Together, the three of them walked down the alleyway towards the tack rooms. As they passed the feed rooms, staff members busy with their daily chores, would stop what they were doing to watch the trio as they made their way down the long passage. To the staff, Mike and Andre had merely become the owners and their bosses over the years; they had seen the pictures and trophies in Andre's office and heard the stories over the years, but the sight of the trio walking side by side through the stable made an impression that reminded them all of the legendary figures the three had once been.

The buzz and the rumors had been running through the stables all morning, ever since Owen had called them all into a meeting in the lounge, telling them of Mike's orders, and of the presence of Alexa Connor. The timing of her arrival and the sudden frenzy of interest in the Friesian mare drove the speculation of who the new rider was going to be and it had sparked the interest of the entire group.

Nearing the door of what had been Alexa's private tack room, Mike and Andre both noticed her fall behind them by several steps as she slowed her pace. Pretending not to notice her reaction Mike and Andre continued towards the general tack room used by the staff. Alexa stopped in front of the door which had once been her sacred space away from the rest of the world. Instead of reaching for the ornate black iron door latch, she just reached up to run her hand against the smooth wooden surface of the door. In all the years, she hadn't even thought about everything she had left behind in that private space. It had seemed the farthest thing from her mind.

"Alexa, are you coming?" she heard Mike's voice calling her and she turned away from the door to catch up to them. Once inside the large tack room, Alexa scanned the walls taking a mental inventory of the equipment.

"Anything that you can't find just let Owen know and he will make a list." Andre stated.

"There is a sign-out sheet on the clipboard by the door," Mike added. And they both watched her face as she is processed the idea of being relegated to using the shared equipment. Her face showed the disappointment and uncertainty that she was feeling. Gone was her bold demeanor, as well as the confidence that she had displayed while challenging Mike in Andre's office earlier. She had seemed to come to life surrounded by the images of the three of them working together as a team.

Guilt stabbed at Andre's heart, knowing Mike had been right in his plan to make it her idea to return to the stable, but feeling the pain of watching her now, seeing the regret in her eyes, was killing him. He seriously hoped that Mike would end the charade soon, or else he would.

Alexa walked over to the racks of saddles and inspected them. "I'll go shopping tomorrow. I don't even have anything that is suitable to wear. I didn't exactly think to pack riding boots and a helmet," Alexa answered Mike sarcastically.

Andre grinned at her tenacity and waited to see how Mike would respond.

"As you wish," Mike replied. "But I really don't see the need for you to go out and purchase equipment for just a couple of months when we already have all you will need here."

"I hope you don't think that I am planning on borrowing, much less wearing, someone else's helmet and boots," Alexa snapped back.

"We are a training center Alexa, I have a deal with several vendors and we keep a stock of new apparel and equipment on hand for sale to our client's as a service. This tack room is just for the staff members," Mike answered her. "There is no need to make a special trip into town when we have anything you might need here." With that said, Mike turned towards the door and with a sweeping motion of his hand, he gestured for Alexa to exit the room first, "After you."

After Alexa and Mike walked out, Andre turned out the lights and pulled the door shut behind him.

Standing in the alleyway, Mike reached into the pocket of his jeans for a key ring and Andre held his breathe knowing full well what Mike was fixing to do. Not knowing how Alexa would react had him feeling very uneasy about the whole situation. Being in his office and looking at all the memories had been one thing, opening this door would

be an entirely different one, and Andre braced himself as he watched her face as she stared at the door.

Mike put the key in the lock and turned it,
but hesitated a moment, before gripping the
wrought iron antique door handle that he had originally had installed when he first built the room.
"You are free to see if you can find anything in here
that suits you," Mike said as he pressed down on
the handle and opened the door.

Mike held the door open for Alexa to walk
in before he reached to turn on the lights.

Andre heard Alexa gasp as the lights came
on, illuminating the room. Alexa stood motionless
in the center of the room while both he and Mike
stood just inside the doorway. Andre watched her as
she slowly scanned the room without moving from
the spot where she was standing. When she reached
up to cover her face with both hands, he saw her
shoulders curl forward and her knees start to bend
as her legs trembled beneath her. With one stride,
Andre was at her side, curling her into his chest as
her rubbed her back, letting her lean on him until
she found her balance.

Mike closed the door to the alleyway outside and crossed the room to stand next to them. Placing a hand on her opposite shoulder, Mike said, "Welcome back kid," and he gently kissed the back of her head.

Nestled between the two of them, Alexa found the strength to open her eyes and look around at the memories that they had so perfectly preserved all these years. Everything was exactly the way she had left it the last time she had walked out. She had not been back in this room since the day they had left for the event in Reno. It was as if all the years in between had never existed.

"I can't believe that you kept it all — everything — it's all here..." Alexa choked, trying to hold back all of the emotions that she has buried in her mind for so long.

CHAPTER 26

Both Mike and Andre had excused themselves giving Alexa time to explore her office in private. Once they had both gone, Alexa reached around the left side of trophy case, flipping the switch to illuminate the glass case. The trophies, medals, ribbons, plaques, and mementos represented all of the years that she had spent working towards one goal; to be the best!

She had almost succeeded but making the Olympic team had eluded her. She had been so close; the accident had ended her pursuit of an elusive gold medal. Instead, she had watched from a hotel room in Paris as her archrival stood on the podium as the medal was hung around her neck.

She had been practicing her freestyle routine for months. Tyler had done all of the music composition and choreography designed to showcase her and Gabri's strengths and she had loved the music the first time that she had heard it. Alexa disliked the pop and contemporary music the most of her competitors preferred.

After months of hard work, she had almost perfected the routine and Gabri glided through the figures effortlessly. Her canter pirouettes and piaffes were almost perfect, and Gabri glided through the half passes and one-times. Together they made an awesome duo.

What had caused Gabri to spook that night was still a mystery to her. It was all just a blur. One minute they were halfway through a beautiful routine, and the next thing she remembered was being loaded into the ambulance She could only remember bits and pieces of the ride to the ER, wavering in and out of consciousness.

It wasn't until they were getting ready to take x-rays that she became fully aware of the situation she was in, and what it meant. As Alexa heard the question, her mind panicked.

"Before we do the x-rays we need to know if there is any possibility that you could be pregnant?"

Her thoughts had immediately gone to her unborn baby. "Yes," Alexa had answered.

"Do you know how far along?"

"About four months…" Fear swamped over Alexa drowning out the excruciating pain of her physical injury as the searing pain in her heart took over. "What about my baby — is he ok — he has to be ok…" Alexa had not known if it was a boy or girl, but she had wanted and wished for a boy and always thought of the baby she was carrying inside of her as a son.

"Take it easy, sweetie. I'm going to be right back…" The nurse had left the room and returned moments later with a fetal heart tone monitor. After several attempts, the faint sound of a heartbeat could be heard and the tears started rolling down Alexa's face. "He is going to be alright," Alexa asked the nurse. But she could see the grim look on the nurses face that sent Alexa into a panic. "He is going to be alright, right? His heart is beating…"

"Let's get the doctor in here to take a look," the nurse answered her as she left Alexa alone in the room, returning a few minutes later with the ER doctor and a portable ultrasound machine.

Everything after that was a complete blur in Alexa's mind. She heard what they had said but couldn't process it all and everything just went blank. They were explaining everything; having her sign consent form after consent form — but the one that she had refused to sign was the one to terminate the pregnancy. Despite the prognosis — despite the facts — despite the complications — she had wanted to give birth to her baby and would not budge on her decision. And to this day, it was the one decision that she did not regret, even for a moment.

Sitting alone in her office, surrounded by all of the trophies, ribbons, awards, medals, and photographs — it was locket resting against her chest that she cherished the most.

CHAPTER 27

At first the staff had been in awe of having Alexa working in the stables but over the course of weeks, the speculation of the relationship between her, Mike and Andre started the rumors.

She was fascinating to watch and the progress that she had made with mare was truly astounding. Under Alexa's handling and training, the mare had literally transformed from the black demon that they had all despised, into an athlete that gave it everything that she had and never quit trying. Alexa had lived up to her reputation.

The younger riders looked up to her in awe and fascination; hanging around just to watch her ride. Most too star-struck to even approach her or ask questions. They were just content to watch. Alexa kept distance from the other riders and trainers and focused all of her attention on the mare.

It was the staff that became keenly perplexed by the interactions between the three former team mates; fueling the speculation of their current relationship to each other after all the years apart.

None would openly suggest, much less question the trio, but amongst themselves, there were many discussions and debates.

There were times when the three of them acted as a single unit and then there were those days when the tension between then could electrify the air, sending the staff heading in the opposite direction.

When Alexa wasn't in the stable she was up at the cabin in her office working on her own business. Mike had taken to spending more time in the training center now that she was back and he and Andre hovered around her like she was made of glass and often engaged in heated debates about the progress that she was making with the mare.

Mike tended to continue to challenge her, while Andre thought Mike was pushing her way too fast. It was something that bewildered the staff as to the reasons why.

Why had she quit riding? What had happened in all the years? Why was she now living in the guesthouse, when she had been spending all of her time with Mike prior to Andre's return?

There had been mention of an accident, but none of them knew the details. At least the mystery of the locked door had been solved.

CHAPTER 27

Andre dialed Alexa's number and listened to it ring, hoping she was still up. When she answered it after only three rings, he breathed a sigh of relief that he hadn't disturbed her.

"Hey Short Stuff, what are you doing?"

"Just working on a new marketing campaign."

"I'm sorry, want me to let you go?"

"No I needed to take a break and give it a rest for the night. I'm glad you called. Gives me an excuse to get my mind off of it for a bit."

"You looked great out there today," Andre said.

"Thank-you, that really means a lot. Still feels awkward to be back riding again."

"I keep wondering what it would have been like if the accident hadn't happened."

"I'm still amazed that you two kept everything exactly the way that I left it," Alexa said. "I sit in there alone and it feels like it never happened."

"I prayed and I hoped every day that you would come back." There was so much that he wanted to say but it felt like he was treading thin ice, not wanting to hear it crack beneath him. I never forgot what it was like between us Alexa."

"I didn't either — I tried — "

"I tried too — all these years — waiting, wondering… Then when I heard you were back…" Andre let the next sentence go unsaid. Finding out about her and Mike had eaten at him like a festering wound.

"Why did you never marry and start a family of your own? I just assumed you would."

"I guess I never clicked with the right one. Alexa you still don't get it. There never was anyone — that made me feel the way I did about you. I don't care about Mike — nothing has changed — nothing can change the way I still feel when I look at you." Andre couldn't let it go. "If you had only told me the real reason that you ended our relationship. Now I can't stop thinking about what it would have been like to have a son — our son."

"Oh Andre, if I could undo all the mistakes that I made I would, in a heartbeat."

"Did you really think I would do to you what Brent had done?"

"Yes…" Alexa got quiet remembering how she had panicked when she had realized that she was pregnant and how her only thought had been to save herself from the heartache of having Andre turn his back on her. She couldn't face that again, so she had broken it off first. At the time it had seemed like the only way out. She knew abortion was never an option she would consider and she didn't know what in the world her next plan would be, but facing Andre with the news was not something she could do either.

The guilt that she felt over losing the baby seemed like a just punishment that she still carried with her and it haunted her dreams every single day.

"Alexa…are you still there?"

"Yes — just thinking…"

"I can hear the gears grinding from here," Andre joked, trying to break the tension.

"I've made so many mistakes in my life. I can't undo the past Andre."

"No one is asking you to Alexa. We all made mistakes that we regret — not being there for you when you needed me the most kills me to think about…"

"I should have told you — I wanted to tell you — I wanted you there — I needed you there — one mistake lead to another mistake — I didn't want to break off our relationship…" Alexa stumbled on her words.

"Shhh babe, just breath and take it easy. I understand now why you didn't. I can't even imagine how you must have been feeling."

"I'm so sorry, sorry for everything. I made a mess of everything…"

"You don't have to apologize — please don't — and you didn't make a mess of everything. I did. I should have known better. I should have figured it out."

"But I hurt you — I hurt Mike — And I lost our baby…" Alexa sobbed. "And I've done it again. I can't ignore my feelings for Mike and what we have shared in the last two years — and I can't deny my feelings for you either."

"And what about us?"

"I won't choose Andre! I can't…"

"Then what the hell are we going to do? I can't live my life without you in it."

"I don't know Andre — I can't live without either of you. No matter what I do, someone is going to get hurt — all three of us — I don't know anything anymore. Except that I am in love with you both and need you both. We were a team; and a damn good one, until I screwed everything up."

"I am on my way down there. I need to see you. I'm not having this conversation on the damn phone when I can see the lights in the cabin from here."

"Andre…" Alexa said, and then heard as the call disconnected.

CHAPTER 28

Mike was just heading up the hill from the stable when he spotted the headlights of Andre's truck. Mike sped up and then eased his truck alongside Andre's, essentially cutting him off from heading towards the cabin.

"Where are you heading at this time of night?" Mike asked, knowing full well where Andre was going.

"Up to the cabin. And where are you heading?" Andre answered him sarcastically.

"Alyssa wasn't answering her phone so I was going up to check on her."

"That's because we were on the phone."

"I kind of figured that…"

"Yeh, well…" Andre answered, getting more aggravated by the minute. Mike was deliberately blocking the access road up to the cabin and it was grating on his already short temper. "Mike, move the damn truck. I am going to finish the conversation that we were having. I'm not playing games on the phone anymore. So move the damn truck!"

"I can't take this shit anymore," Mike answered, but didn't take the truck out of park.

"Well if you don't move the damn truck you won't have to worry about it."

"What the hell is that supposed to mean."

"She is seriously considering packing and leaving for good and if she does, there won't be any changing her mind this time, that's what it means. So are you going to get the hell out of my way or what?"

"She can't be serious."

"Oh she is dead serious," Andre answered.

"What happened? She seemed to be settling in, was back riding, and seemed happy being back home. I don't get it." Mike questioned.

"She won't choose between us. She'd rather leave then feel like she is betraying either of us."

"What?"

"She is not stupid Mike. And we aren't teenagers anymore. We both want her for our own and she wants and needs us both and she will not choose one over the over. Ending it and leaving is the only solution she can see as possible. She is tired of denying her own feelings to make us happy."

I am going up to the cabin whether I have to go around you or through you so I suggest you move the damn truck," Andre threatened Mike and meant it.

"Well then it looks we are heading in the same direction because this isn't over and I am going up there too.

"Be my guest, but get out of my damn way, now!

"Alexa heard the two trucks pull up right behind each other and she knew that meant trouble. She had told Andre how she felt and now Mike was in tow. There wasn't going to be an easy way out of this mess they had all created. The pair barged in the front door demanding answers that he couldn't give them. She had said all she could say. She may be wrong for feeling the way that she did but it was the truth. She couldn't separate the way that she felt about of them. She loved them both and was in love with the both. She loved them both and for different reasons, denying her feelings and feeling guilty for betraying either one was something she couldn't do. And as long as she stayed at the ranch, they would both constantly wonder and doubt her loyalty if she did choose.

"I swear, if you both don't stop it right now, I mean it, I am getting on a flight in the morning and it is over. I can't do this. I can't live like this." Alexa slammed her glass down on the butcher block island hard enough to leave an indention in the wooden surface. "Haven't we all made enough mistakes to last a lifetime?"

Both Mike and Andre froze. Alexa might only be a fraction of their size but when she was this angry she could be like a keg of dynamite and they both knew that her words were no threat. The last thing either of them wanted was to lose her again, and this time it would be forever.

""Why should I have to choose? I am sick and tired of pretending. — Pretending that I am someone that I am not. — Sick of the lies and sick of trying to pretend that the past doesn't matter. — Sick and tired of trying to deny the feelings and love that I have in my heart for both of you. I won't choose between you both. — I won't! I can't! — And if that means leaving you both, than I will. I have done it before, I'll do it again. I'll live with the good memories of how it was, rather than stay here and be pulled between you. Now it is the two of you that will have to choose. What do you want? What do you both want from me?" Having vented her anger and left feeling completely drained and numb, Alexa grabbed her glass and headed to the kitchen to fix another drink, leaving them both standing there looking shell shocked.

Alone in the kitchen, Alexa leaned up against the granite counter top. She meant what she had said. She couldn't five them both what they wanted, and she couldn't deny her feelings for either. Her whole life she had always had to deny her true feelings to suit everyone else's needs. She was tired of living the lies and running from the truth. Inside her heart was shattering all over again at the thought of losing both of them again. The thought of having to leave it all behind once more was killing her.

"What the hell do we do now?" Mike said, running his hands through his hair trying to make sense of it all. He couldn't deny how much he loved her and he couldn't stand the thought of losing her again, not now, not ever and he knew in his heart that Andre felt the same.

"Beats the shit out of me," Andre said as he turned towards the window to stare out at the inky darkness that mirrored the hole in his heart at the thought of not having her in his life. "I won't let her go — I can't!"

"I know." Mike answered.

CHAPTER 29

Alexa was softly moaning in her sleep as she curled up tighter into Mike's arms. Her head nestled into the crook of his arm, her long wavy hair fanned out on the pillow between them, Alexa begin to stir as the sleepy fog of morning begin to lift, arousing her senses, bringing with it the need to stretch out the kinks.

The faint morning light was just beginning to illuminate the wall of glass that separated the master bedroom from the outside balcony. Alexa slowly turned over and quietly disentangled her body from his arms as she slipped out of his embrace and out of the bed they shared.

Some things had never changed. Alexa was usually the first one up in the morning. She loved the early morning sunrise and would quietly slip out of bed and make her way to the kitchen. Making her first cup of coffee, she arranged a plate of fresh fruit, cheese and a boiled egg then headed out with her breakfast to the terrace to enjoy the sunrise.

Still in a wonderful sleepy daze from their night of beautiful lovemaking, Alexa propped her feet up on the chair on the opposite side of the wrought iron table, stretching her legs and enjoying the first sip of her morning coffee.

As the sun slowly started to glow just over the horizon Alexa nibbled at the fresh fruit on the plate. She loved the taste of the cool melon as it contrasted with the warmth of the coffee.

The sunrise, with its beautiful hues and colors brightening the horizon, always brought with it the clean fresh promise of a brand new day.

Alexa felt his soft touch as his arms slid around her shoulders gently tipping her chin up before covering her lips with his.

"Good Morning Sunshine."

"Good Morning Beautiful," Alexa answered him.

"I am so happy that you are home," Andre said as he set his coffee mug on the table next to hers.

"So am I," Alexa said as she kissed his arm. "So am I."

"I'll never understand why you two find it so necessary to wake the dead before the chickens are even up in the morning," Mike said as he set his coffee mug on the table.

"Good morning to you too, sleepyhead," Alexa replied.

Against all the odds, the three of them were back together again. Somehow they had managed to sort through their differences and get over the obstacles that stood in their way of true happiness. Their relationship may not be for everyone, but it was the only option for them. Without each other they had realized that none of them would ever be truly happy.

Dear Reader, I hope you enjoyed the first book in the Free to Be Me Series. I'd love it if you could post a review about it on Amazon or book websites. Getting reviews for my books lets me know what my readers enjoyed most about my books, and I look forward to reading what you think. Perhaps you can mention who your favorite character is, and which parts you like best. If you've spotted a typo, email me at alyssa.tanner.author@gmail.com. You can also follow me on Twitter where my user name is @AlyssaT_author. I look forward to hearing from you.

Best Wishes and Kind Regards,

Alyssa Tanner